A *Very* Practical Guide to Discipline with Young Children

A *Very* Practical Guide to Discipline with Young Children

by
Dr. Grace L. Mitchell

REVISED EDITION

Telshare Publishing, Inc. • *West Palm Beach, FL*

International Standard Book Number 0–910287–12–0

REVISED EDITION

First Printing June, 1998

Illustrations by Sylvia Feinburg

Table of Contents

Dedication ix

Acknowledgments xi

Foreword xiii

Chapter 1: The Three Main Themes of This Book 1

The I AM! I CAN! Philosophy 1
Definition of Discipline 2
A Four Step Plan of Action 3

Chapter 2: Anticipate and Avoid Trouble 5

Orderly Transitions 7
What Are Your Zero Hours? 8

Chapter 3: Hesitate Before You Act 13

Count to Ten 13
Buy Some Time 14

Chapter 4: Investigate the Cause 17

Seeking Clues to Behavior in the Child Care Center 17
PEOPLE 18
ENVIRONMENT 18
PROGRAM 19
Parents Can Use the Same Approach 21

**Chapter 5: Communicate — Open the Doors
of Understanding** 23

Listening to Your Child 24
Teaching Communication Skills 25
"Talk-It-Over" Chairs 26
Pouring Fuel on the Flames 28

Chapter 6: Basic Trust   33

  Trust is the Core of Relationships   34
  Parents Are Not Always Perfect   34
  Child Abuse Isn't Always Physical   35
  Love, Respect and Consistency   35

Chapter 7: Parents Are Teachers   37

  I'll Teach You   37
  No Cookbook Recipes   39
  Halos of Heroes   40

Chapter 8: Doing What Comes Naturally   41

  Eating in the Home   42
  A Touch of Class   43
  Table Manners   44
  Eating in the Child Care Center   45
  You Can't Win   45
  Eliminating   46
  Sleeping   48
  Dressing and Washing   50
  A Sense of Order   52

Chapter 9: Behavior That Bugs You   53

  Biting   53
  Lying   56
  Truth is Stranger Than Fiction   57
  Why Do They Tell Lies?   59
  Stealing   61
  Unacceptable Language   62
  Bathroom Talk   65
  Throwing   66
  Temper Tantrums   68

Chapter 10: Move Over for the New Baby   73

How Would You Feel?   74
Delayed Feelings of Jealousy   75
Covering Up Jealousy   77
Make the Child Part of the Planning   79

Chapter 11: Grown-Ups Goof Too   83

Making Threats You Can't Carry Out   84
Out on a Limb   85
Offering Choices When There Are No Choices   86
The "Put Down" Destroys the I AM!   87
Comparison and Competition   89
Bribes and Rewards   90
Gold Stars   91
Manners   91
Demanding Apologies   92
Nagging and Scolding   95

Chapter 12: Call in the Reserves   97

Don't Hesitate to Ask for Help   97
*Parents and Teachers Need to Understand
    Each Other*   99
Report Something Positive   99
Don't Try to "Wing It" Alone   101

Chapter 13: Some Thoughts on Punishment   103

Spanking   103
Verbal Abuse   105
Fair and Equal   106
Wearing Two Hats   107
Isolation and Separation   110
The "Thinking Chair"   111
Withdrawal of Privileges   112

Chapter 14: An Ounce of Prevention   115

Bring the Feelings Out in the Open   116
The Pressure Cooker   117
Dictating Stories and Poems   117
Puppets   119
A Punching Bag   119
Pounding   122
Painting is More Than Art   123
Helping a Child Talk Out Problems   124
Water Play — the Most Accessible Material   125
Reading and Telling Stories   125
Music   126
Dramatic Play Discloses Feelings   126

Chapter 15: A Piece of the Action   129

The Wallace Corporation — A Family Meeting   129
Allowances   131
Democracy in the Classroom   134
Cassette Recorders and Message Centers   136

Chapter 16: Wrong Way! Turn Back!   139

A Plan for Change   140
Look at Your Own I AM   140
How Were You Disciplined?   141
*What Kind of Adults Do You Want Your
    Children to Be?*   142
It's Later Than You Think!   143

Chapter 17: In a Nutshell   145

Index   147

About the Author   153

This book is dedicated to my children, who served as guinea pigs for my own growth, and to my grandchildren, who have tested the advice offered here in bringing up another generation.

Acknowledgments

To the people who read my manuscript and offered helpful suggestions for the first edition, I am still grateful.

For this second edition, I wish to acknowledge the influence of Karen Miller, a prolific author of books for teachers of young children, and known worldwide as a public speaker. Our mutual interest in early childhood education has led to a long lasting friendship.

I offer special thanks...

...to Nancy Bailey, for managing the process from outlining the changes to producing this revised edition;

...to Maria Occhippinti, who read this updated manuscript from the point of view of a young mother in our present society;

...to Francine Hayward, a writer and mother of three children;

...and most especially to Lois Dewsnap, who spent the greater part of her vacation working on the details of reorganizing and updating material.

Foreword

When this book was first published, it was based on the experiences of a teacher, mother and grandmother. The true stories told here emerged from the feelings which were expressed by children through their second language, behavior. I expected adults to interpret them from their own perspective, and perhaps to find new options for action.

In 1998, it is gratifying to know, through hundreds of letters, that my words have influenced many parents and teachers who have developed a new understanding of why children do what they do.

That they have found a new measure of joy in living and learning with their children is my reward.

A *Very* Practical
Guide to Discipline
with Young Children

CHAPTER 1

The Three Main Themes of This Book

The I AM! I CAN! Philosophy

The basic philosophy which undergirds everything I think, teach and practice in my daily life can be stated in four short words, I AM! I CAN!

In this diagram, the square represents a human being, one

who is growing, developing, changing, from the moment of his birth, in four ways. Physically, as bones and muscles develop; socially, as a member of an ever-enlarging community; intellectually, as the computer in his brain takes in and spits out more information; and emotionally, as he is learning to cope with the strains and stresses encountered in everyday life.

When the I AM is strong — when a person feels good about herself — self-confidence allows her to venture, to take risks, and to attempt new feats, whether it be the infant taking her first steps or the mountain climber. If she reaches her goal, her I CAN expands.

"I did it! I did it! I DID IT!" I shouted, and wrote to all my friends when I earned my Ph.D. I know what it means to have your I AM stretch and grow, and I have discovered that with each achievement a door opens to another exciting experience. The I AM feeds the I CAN, which in turn reinforces the I AM, and a positive circular motion falls into place.

Teachers and parents who are in daily contact with children need to be constantly aware of the subtle ways in which they can influence the positive motion of the "I AM! I CAN!" They should also be conscious of the ways in which they can put that motion in reverse. They do it with the put-down: "How stupid can you get?" Humiliation: "So you'll wear diapers until you can act like a big girl." Rejection: "Walk behind me. I don't want anyone to know such a scruffy looking kid belongs to me," and with all the cruel, hurtful things adults sometimes say which make a child feel, "I'm no good! I can't do anything right."

Recently I have read of research which indicates that the antisocial behavior we deplore — cheating, lying, bullying, destroying property, defiance, fighting, friction with peers and teachers and worse — stems from the poor self-image imposed on children in their early years.

The I AM! I CAN! philosophy works! You can call it self-confidence, or competency, or whatever words you choose, but the theory remains constant. The most important thing you can do for a child is to help him hold his head high — I AM; reach out for the stars — I CAN; and know the sweet satisfaction of success.

Definition of Discipline

What are the words that pop into your mind when you think of discipline?

Obedience? Punishment? Making kids behave?

How often we hear people say, "That kid is spoiled....His parents never discipline him."

"She wouldn't be such a brat if she got a little discipline."

"That teacher has poor discipline. Her kids walk all over her."

"Kids today don't know the meaning of discipline."

For most people, the word discipline has a negative

connotation. It implies someone is going to tighten the thumbscrews. Parents or teachers are obligated to do something to a child, just as the law and courts do something to recalcitrant adults.

What I propose here is a plan of action which will ultimately lead to self-discipline. My plan presupposes that the adults who try to follow it in their dealings with young children will, themselves, have achieved some measure of self-discipline. It also makes the assumption, based on a growing body of scientific evidence, that from the earliest stages of life a child is a thinking, feeling human being, and that our task is to help him develop into a competent, self-confident adult. To that end, I have developed the following definition, which puts the adult in the role of advisor and helper, ready to step in and rescue the child from mistakes which will harm him physically or emotionally, but willing to let him make the mistakes which will enable him to grow:

Discipline is the slow, bit by bit, time consuming task of helping children to see the sense in acting in a certain way.

This definition is the core of everything that follows, and I will be making frequent references to it throughout the book.

A Four Step Plan of Action

The key words in my plan of action are:

ANTICIPATE

HESITATE

INVESTIGATE

COMMUNICATE

These four steps cannot always be separated into neat compartments. In some of the anecdotes in the following chapters, one is more obvious than another, but often they are all present to some extent. As you read, you will find them mentioned again and again, and each time they will bring new insights to your own understanding of the goals of discipline.

CHAPTER 2

Anticipate and Avoid Trouble

As Mrs. Thomas pulled into the driveway, she noticed that her son's car was in the other side of the garage. David is home early, she thought. Her cheerful greeting died on her lips when she saw her son lying on the couch, staring despondently at the ceiling.

"What's wrong?" she asked anxiously.

David sat up and forced a smile. "Nothing serious. I had a lousy day with the kids in my preschool class and I am wondering whether this is the right career for me. Sometimes I think I am a darned good teacher, but on a day like this I think I'm not doing these kids much good, and they sure don't do anything for my ego!"

Mrs. Thomas sank into her favorite easy chair and kicked off her shoes. "Tell me about it," she invited as she massaged one foot with the toes of the other. "Was it one special incident or the whole day?"

Her tall, rangy son stood up and walked around the room as he talked. "Well, it really began at snack time," he said. "We had a good morning up 'til then. That old briefcase I took in set up a whole new chain of activities. They set up an office near the housekeeping corner and were really involved in dramatic play. And then when we were having snack we had great conversation. But when we were through, I said, 'O.K., now we are going out on the playground' and you would think I had pushed a button that set off a cyclone. They all jumped up and made a mad dash for the door. Anton bumped into

5

Jacques who turned around and punched him, yelling, 'You knocked me down, you dummy!' Of course Anton hit back, and then some of the other kids got into it and all of a sudden I had a first rate fight on my hands. A couple of little girls got scared and began to cry, and just at that moment Liz (the director) walked in with a visitor. I got the kids together as fast as I could and took them outside. Liz left early so I didn't hear about it today, but I expect I will tomorrow when we have our conference."

Mrs. Thomas smiled sympathetically. "That was this morning. Was the rest of the day so bad?"

"Yeah, that's where my doubts come in. I should have been able to get things back under control, but it seems as if they were out to get me for the rest of the day. Three kids spilled their milk at lunch. I had a hassle with that new kid, Enrico — he called me a fancy four-letter name when I told him to clean up the mess he had made. No one slept at rest, and I lost my patience and yelled at them! The whole afternoon just seemed to tell me I am not temperamentally suited to work with little kids. They are learning all the wrong things from me."

Mrs. Thomas continued with what seemed to be an irrelevant question. "Does the school have a plan for evacuating the children in case of fire?"

David looked at her, puzzled and somewhat annoyed. "Of course."

"Do you have fire drills to test your plan?"

"Certainly!"

"Well, someone had to think that plan out from beginning to end, **ANTICIPATE** all of the possible dangers, and then test them. Now let's go back and look at the incident that gave you so much grief and see what kind of planning you could have done.

"Remember, you have only been a full-fledged teacher for two months. When you were in training there was always someone standing by to coach you through a rough time. By now I guess you know that your real education began after you graduated and started to put all that book learning into practice. As a former teacher, I have news for you. The learning process never stops. When you work with growing, living, human beings they will continue to teach you as much as you teach them. Some of it adds up to plain common sense but most of it is through trial and error."

"I can agree with your theory," David said, "but I thought you were going to tell me what I did that was wrong."

"I intend to try," she responded with a smile. "It sounds as if you failed to **ANTICIPATE**."

Orderly Transitions

"What do you mean by that?" he asked, with a thoughtful frown.

"While you were still sitting at the table you should have been thinking, 'When we finish with our snack we are going outside. How am I going to move this group of kids from here to there in an orderly fashion?'

"Then you could have quietly and matter-of-factly said, 'In a few minutes when everyone is through, we are going outside. First I need two helpers to clean up the table. Petra and Jerry, you may do it today. Be sure to get the dustpan and brush and sweep up the crumbs under the table and take a sponge and wipe the table top. Charlie, you pick up the cups and put them into the waste basket, and Sally, you may take the cracker basket back to the kitchen. The rest of us are going to get our jackets. Now all the people who have something blue on may go first.

"Making an orderly transition from one activity to another is an acquired skill," she went on, "but when you learn it, your problems with group management will be greatly diminished. When you abruptly say, 'We are going out,' with no forewarning, you are practically inviting them to stampede!"

"I see what you mean," David grinned, feeling better already. "Did you learn all that when you were a teacher? Seems to me that you practiced some of it when we were kids. Can you really think of two things simultaneously?"

"Sure," his mother answered, "I do it all the time. I suspect that you do, too. You just haven't been aware of it. As to when you were little, yes, I had to learn to plan ahead. For instance, if I said at the breakfast table, 'I think we will go to the beach today,' you might not have knocked me over on your way out the door, but I would have found myself with a table full of dirty dishes. Instead I would give out the directions.

'David will clear the table and load the dishwasher. Lucille can mix up some tuna salad and make sandwiches. Dan, you make a gallon of lemonade, and when you have all made your beds and finished your jobs, we will take off.'"

David laughed delightedly. "Of course! I remember those assignments, but I didn't realize then that you were manipulating us. You're really something, Mum! Thanks for the tip. I can't wait now to get back to the center to try it out!"

What Are Your Zero Hours?

Think about your "zero hours." We all have them, that time in the day when everything is just "too much." When my children were small and I was doubling as a breadwinner and parent, the hour between 5:00 and 6:00 p.m. was my Waterloo. It seemed as though my children always chose the time when I was trying to get dinner to make demands, "I have to have $5.00 tomorrow," or to blame me, "You forgot to put any dessert in my lunch today," or to tattle on each other, "Bill had to go to the principal's office!" That was when they squabbled or teased each other until someone dissolved into tears. One day I called them together and made an announcement. "I am giving you fair warning," I stated. "I have had a rough day. I am tired and hungry and I am as cross as a bear. If you are smart you will find something to do and keep out of my way!" They looked at me with shocked surprise which turned to sympathy. It worked, at least that time! Lee went down into the cellar to his workshop. Nancy offered to play a game of checkers with her brother Bill. By the time we sat down to dinner, I was able to relax and smile again. I praised them for their cooperation and rewarded them with their favorite dessert. That was a case when I learned that it "makes sense to act in a certain way."

Mrs. Fitzgerald, the young mother in our next story, found her zero hour at a different time. A single parent, working to support her four-year-old son, she had no relatives or close friends nearby to call upon for help or guidance. Every Thursday (pay day), she took Michael with her to the supermarket while she shopped for the coming week.

"Michael Fitzgerald, you put that back on the shelf and come right here!"

Vicki Stanton, the director of a child care center, was shopping for her family in the supermarket when she heard Mrs. Fitzgerald shrieking at her four-year-old son. She had witnessed several scenes between this volatile little boy and his mother and she did not want to get drawn into this one, so she quickly moved an aisle away, but she could not help hearing the continuing hassle.

"Move when I call you or you'll get it when we go home," his mother shouted. Michael only grinned, carefully keeping out of reach. This was a favorite game, and he knew he could win. He glanced around, and seeing that he had an interested audience, he stuck his fingers in his ears and waved them at his mother, mocking her with a derisive "N'ya, N'ya, N'ya!"

The scenario continued until Michael's mother, finished with her shopping, caught him and dragged him out the door screaming and crying. The last thing Vicki heard was Michael's angry shout, "You twisted my arm! Stop hurting me, you old fart!"

The following Monday a shamefaced mother sought help from Vicki.

"I saw you in the supermarket Thursday," she said. "I was so embarrassed! I hate to take Michael shopping with me but I have no one to leave him with. He just waits until we get where he knows everyone is looking at us, and then he starts to show off!"

"I saw that you were having a hard time," Vicki said quietly. "I'm sure many people were sympathizing with you but you probably felt that they were all criticizing you for being a bad mother."

"Yes, that is exactly how I felt," this frustrated mother went on, relieved to find that someone understood. "Michael makes me feel so stupid. Here I am, a grown woman, and that little guy gets the better of me every time."

"Parenting isn't all fun and games," Vicki answered. "Children can be so sweet one minute and drive us right up the wall a moment later."

"But maybe if I had more education I would know how to deal with Mike," Mrs. Fitzgerald went on. "You teachers never seem to have the problems we do."

"Oh yes, we do," Vicki replied, "but we have several advantages. If we have had a bad day, we can look forward to walking away from the situation. You can't. We try to do our best for your child but the real responsibility falls on your shoulders, and that is never-ending.

"Even more important, we have a support system which you are lacking. If Mike gives his teacher a hard time she can call on me, or one of the other teachers will step in and divert his attention.

"Also, think about the environment here. Everything is planned to make life comfortable for children. Even the furniture is scaled down to their size. We can provide Mike with a place and program which fits his needs. When he goes with you into an adult world, he has to conform to a different set of standards.

"Now I suggest that before you to go the market again, you **ANTICIPATE**."

"Oh, I do," Mrs. Fitzgerald said with a wry grin, "and how I dread it!"

Vicki smiled and went on. "That wasn't exactly what I meant," she said. "As you **ANTICIPATE** the problem, look for ways to avoid it. You are tired and hungry when you pick up Michael on Thursday, but so is he. To you the shopping is a necessary chore. To Michael, it's a matter of trailing after you when he'd much rather be someplace else. He's not only tired and hungry, he's also bored. He wants your attention, and instead it's on the grocery list. It's not surprising that he acts up.

"Suppose you make Michael a partner. On Wednesday night, make out your list together. Give him some choices about which fruits or vegetables you are going to buy, and let him choose one kind of cookies or snacks. Then when you get to the store, let him find some of the items, matching labels and box fronts. We play all kinds of matching games at school — it's part of our reading readiness program — and Mike is very good at it. Just think how proud he would feel if he could demonstrate this to you in a useful way.

"Be sure to offer him the reward of praise when he does something helpful. For example:

"'Michael, you were such a help to me, pushing the cart, carrying the bundles and putting the food away. After we eat, how about a story?'"

"That makes a lot of sense," exclaimed Mrs. Fitzgerald. "And maybe Mike and I could go eat someplace before we shop. He'd love that."

"Good idea," agreed Vicki. "One thing more, though. All your problems aren't going to clear up in one shopping trip. Before you go out again, sit down and talk to Michael. Tell him how you feel when he misbehaves. Tell him what will happen if it occurs again, and be sure to follow through. Consistency is one of the most important keys to behavior management. It is part of the security children are seeking. Good luck, and let me know what happens."

We cannot foresee all of life's problems but when we know where the trouble spots are, we can learn to **ANTICIPATE** and plan ahead.

CHAPTER 3

Hesitate Before You Act

Count to Ten

Joseph, an intelligent but emotionally high-strung child, stood glaring defiantly at his teacher. With a wild display of temper Joseph had destroyed a new game, thrown a chair across the room, narrowly missing two other children, and shouted a string of obscenities at Mrs. Carruthers. It was the third such demonstration in one week, and she was at her wit's end. Her face was crimson with suppressed anger — his, alternately taunting and frightened. "I need to buy a little time," she thought in desperation. "If I touch him I may hurt him — I am so angry!" Joseph, waiting for her to make the next move, was taken by surprise when she turned her back on him. Her twisting hands and white knuckles spoke of her feelings more loudly than words could have; even Joseph's youthful eyes couldn't fail to get the message. Finally, she turned around and in controlled tones said, "You know, Joseph, there are times when you make me so angry that I feel like YELLING at you," raising her voice to a shout. "Or I want to GRAB you and SHAKE YOU HARD," and she demonstrated with violent shaking movements but did not actually touch him. Joseph was awestruck. She had his full attention.

"But of course," she went on, "I can't do either of those things. I am a grown-up, and a teacher. I have to learn to control my feelings! So I turned my back and took very deep breaths and counted to ten. You could see that it was hard —

but if I hadn't done that I might have hurt you!

"The last time you had one of these awful temper tantrums, you told me you could feel them coming on."

Joseph, thoroughly intrigued by now, and flattered to be the object of her attention, nodded in agreement.

"Yeah, it's like you said. It's like when the first rumblings of thunder warn us that a storm is coming."

"Well, you had to be intelligent to understand that," Mrs. Carruthers continued, "but you aren't being very smart when you fail to get the message! Your mind is supposed to tell your body what to do, but you are letting your body be the boss and tell your mind what to do. Instead of your brain making decisions, your arms and legs are in control, and they get you into trouble every time!

"Do you suppose my method could work for you? When you feel a temper tantrum coming on, could you take ten deep breaths? Like this...let's try it."

Together they took ten very deep breaths.

"There, that was good," Mrs. Carruthers said with an approving smile. "Now you see that if you could do that it would buy you some time, give your brain a chance to tell your body, 'Hey, I'm in control here. I will be the boss! I will decide what you are going to do!'"

Joseph was still cautiously suspicious, but the idea of being the "boss" obviously intrigued him.

At this point, Mrs. Carruthers could almost see the wheels turning in Joseph's mind. She had given him a fascinating new idea — that he could be the BOSS of his own actions. It was obvious that his keen and absorbent mind was in high gear when he went back to his desk.

By **HESITATING**, Mrs. Carruthers accomplished two things. She gave herself time to cool her anger and approach Joseph in a calm and persuasive manner. She was also teaching Joseph, through her example and her specific suggestions, the value of stopping to think before acting.

Buy Some Time

When, in spite of your best efforts, you find yourself in the middle of a behavior problem, try to buy a little time. Turn your back. Walk away. Or just stand there looking intently and directly at the child. This lack of immediate action is often a surprise which catches a child off guard. It may change his train of thought from "I'll get her!" to "What is she going to do?" and in that few seconds you may change yours from, "Darn that kid! He's doing it to me again!" to "What can be going on within this child that makes him feel so mean?"

Ann, the director of a child care center, told this story. "Last Friday was the pits! It had rained for two days; the cook called in sick at the last moment; I had three substitutes in that day and when I called Mrs. Fraser to tell her Sammy had an earache, she didn't come for him for three hours. I let myself get drawn into a hassle with one of the kids who deliberately threw some paint at Harvey Jackson but instead of hitting Harvey it spattered all over the wall. I told him to clean it up and he looked at me and said, 'I won't and you can't make me! Harvey started the fight. Make him clean it up!'

"I'll admit I felt like swatting him, but of course I couldn't. My next thought was, he's right. I can't make him do it. He's a big strong kid and I'm not going to try to force him. What CAN I do? To buy myself some time I stooped down so we were face to face, held him firmly by the shoulders, and looked him right in the eyes. He was surprised, waiting to see what I was going to do to him. I still didn't know, so I took my time, and then a funny thing happened. It seemed so ridiculous — the two of us staring at each other — that the corners of my mouth began to twitch. He grinned just a little bit, still not sure of what was going on, and in another second we both burst out laughing.

"The tension was broken. I said, 'O.K., I didn't see what happened. I don't know who was to blame. Get a pan of water and some sponges and I will help you clean up.'

"'I'll help too,' Harvey chimed in, and the two of them cleaned it up, buddies again. The day was saved!"

CHAPTER 4

Investigate the Cause

Mrs. Carruthers did not stop with the suggestions she planted in Joseph's mind (in Chapter 3). She moved on with the third step in my plan — **INVESTIGATE**.

It may be helpful for parents to understand the steps that are likely to be taken in a child care center.

Seeking Clues to Behavior in the Child Care Center

First, Mrs. Carruthers checked into Joseph's family situation. In a conference with his mother she discovered that his father had died when he was two years old, and that since then he had been the only "man" in the house. Recently his mother had remarried. He was no longer the "king" and the power he had always been able to exert over his mother with temper tantrums and sulking was no longer effective. To make matters worse, his new stepfather brought two sons with him, both older and stronger than Joseph. They had been given his room, and he had been required to move into a much smaller one. It was plain to see that this child was hurting and knowing this helped his teacher to understand some of his behavior. Small wonder that the notion of "being the boss" had been attractive!

In the child care center, when the behavior of a child becomes a constant source of irritation, a wise caregiver could ask her director or supervisor to help her look for clues in the following areas:

PEOPLE

ENVIRONMENT

PROGRAM

PEOPLE

First, she can see what information about his family is available. Does he live with both parents? Do they both work? Has he any brothers or sisters? Is he the youngest, the eldest, or a middle child? Has he recently been displaced by a new baby.? If that information is not enough, the director may ask additional questions such as, "Has there been a major shake-up in the family recently? Is some close family member seriously ill? Has there been a recent death of a beloved relative, or of a pet? Has the child been involved in or witnessed an accident? Has the family moved recently?" These are sensitive questions and the inquirer must tread lightly, ready to back off at the slightest sign of resentment.

The director can also talk to the various individuals who may observe or care for this child in the course of a day. If she encounters conflicting opinions, if one person finds him an interesting, intelligent child, and another describes him as a "fresh, smart-talking brat," the problem may be a conflict between the child and a particular teacher.

ENVIRONMENT

Next, in her search for evidence, the caregiver may look at the ENVIRONMENT. The standards we set for children's behavior must be based on what we know of their developmental needs. When our expectations are contrary to their natural instincts, something has to give. In the child care center we may have become so "accustomed to the place" that we fail to see where we have created a problem. For example, if the furnishings are so arranged that there are long corridors, we waste our energy when we constantly admonish, "No running!" A simple solution is to set up some dividers to break up that space and remove the temptation.

Sometimes it helps to invite an outsider to observe in the center, paying particular attention to the ENVIRONMENT. Or it can be made the subject of a staff meeting. I personally recall one such meeting where the pre-announced topic was Discipline. Each participant was asked to describe a child who was giving her trouble, and the rest of the group offered suggestions.

"I have a wild bunch of four-year-olds," one teacher stated. "They are noisy and rough and destructive."

"Could it be something in the environment?" one of her colleagues asked.

A barrage of questions followed:

"Do you have enough equipment to keep everyone occupied?"

"Is it easily accessible?"

"Do you have an orderly system so children put things back when they have finished with them?"

"Do you give children tools that work?"

"Do the scissors really cut?"

"Is the hammer heavy enough to pound a nail?"

"We talk about encouraging children to have good ideas and to be creative, but we sometimes frustrate them because we don't give them the proper tools!"

"When you are checking the environment, don't forget to look for soft, quiet places where a child can be alone," was the last comment.

It was safe to assume that each one of those teachers went back to look at her own center with a critical eye, and that she may have found in the ENVIRONMENT some answers to the problems of discipline.

PROGRAM

The problem-solving teacher next turns to PROGRAM. Sometimes we impose rigid routines for no better reason than

because we have always done it that way. Each day is just like the one before. Play must end promptly at ten o'clock because it is time for snack. We drag children away from an activity in which they may have been thoroughly engrossed without asking ourselves if it makes sense.

I was visiting in a center when the teacher brought out a new manipulative game, a set of interlocking plastic frames. Four little girls sat down at a table and played with them contentedly. One by one, three of them drifted away to play elsewhere, but Jessie was completely absorbed. Her involvement was so intense that she did not even look up when the teacher announced it was time for juice. At the end of an hour, she rose with a sigh of satisfaction, carefully put the pieces back in the box, placed the box on the shelf, and joined the other children who were now listening to a story. I was impressed with the wisdom and understanding of that teacher who let Jessie stay with her new interest.

Marveling at her staying power, I asked, "Does she always get so involved with that type of activity?"

"Quite the contrary," was the reply. "She normally spends most of her time in dramatic play, and she seldom stays with anything for more than fifteen minutes. This was a side of Jessie we have never seen before which is why I couldn't think of disturbing her! It would have been a shame to break in on that marvelous concentration!"

Parents Can Use the Same Approach

Can these same methods apply in the home? Can a parent who is struggling with a particular behavior problem seek answers by looking at the PEOPLE, ENVIRONMENT, and her daily schedule or PROGRAM? I believe that the answer is yes.

Recently I met with a small group of young mothers who wanted to talk about discipline. The problems they described were the usual ones. "My little girl bites me. It hurts. What shall I do? Should I bite her back?"

"My three-year-old is driving me nuts. He persists in jumping off the back of the big chair in the living room."

"I can't make my two-year-old stop pulling the lamp cord out at the base plugs. I have scolded and spanked, and he still goes right on. All the time I am telling him not to touch he looks me right in the eye and does it again."

As we discussed the three points to **INVESTIGATE** — PEOPLE, ENVIRONMENT and PROGRAM — each of these mothers began to see that there was more than one way to look for solutions.

The first mother may have had a PEOPLE problem. She was advised to note what happened just prior to each biting incident to see whether there was a consistent pattern. Was it when another adult came into the picture, either in person or on the phone? Was her child asking for more attention? Rebelling against correction?

It was plain to see that the lively three-year-old-boy was just "doing what comes naturally" at that age. His mother could use chairs or a table tipped over, a card-table with a blanket thrown over it, a step stool, some pillows and cardboard cartons to create an obstacle course which would give him legitimate opportunities to crawl through, climb over and under, and jump off.

The simplest solution for the third mother was to unplug the lamp during the day and to keep her child's prying fingers out of the plugs with protective covers. In her anxiety to be a good mother she felt that giving in to him would create problems later. She saw it as her duty to "make him mind." She was also urged to be prepared with interesting alternatives when she came smack up against this child's will.

And so **INVESTIGATE** is the third step in our plan. When all is said and done, when rules are made, and a plan is in operation, it then becomes necessary to **COMMUNICATE**.

CHAPTER 5

Communicate — Open the Doors of Understanding

The simplest, most readily available tool we have in dealing with our children is the ability to **COMMUNICATE** with spoken words rather than physical force. Language is the oil which lubricates the journey through life. Words enable us to make our feelings known, to ask for what we need, to explain what we mean, to pass on information, and to offer support and encouragement to others. On the negative side, words can act as weapons. They can inflict emotional damage more lasting than a physical blow. They can also arouse confusion in the young child's mind.

"Our little girl is growing up. She's going to be four years old next Sunday," Leda reminded her husband.

"Can you believe it? Gina is getting so big. She's going to be four next Sunday!" Leda said in her daily phone chat with her mother.

"My little sister is having a birthday! She's going to be four," Gina's sister Maria proudly announced to her friend.

Gina heard all this, and the happy expression on her face made it clear that she was looking forward to the occasion, but no one could have guessed what was in her mind. Sunday came, and Leda was in the kitchen cooking Gina's favorite breakfast — sausages and pancakes — when piercing screams from above sent her flying up the stairs.

"What is it? What happened? Are you hurt?" she called to Gina who was scrunched up on her bed holding up her hands.

"It's Sunday, and I'm not four!"

"Why of course you are. Why do you say that?"

"Because my hands are still small," was the woeful reply.

We can never be certain about the interpretation children will make of the words they hear adults say.

Listening to Your Child

Communication is a two-way street. You expect a child to listen to you, but how well do you listen to her? Really listen! Even a very young child knows when you only pretend to pay attention to what she is saying. If you nod your head, answering with an occasional word or grunt, while your mind is occupied, her radar system will tell her. When you put her off with:

"Don't bother me now. Can't you see I am busy?"

"Go tell your father."

"That's nice."

she will quickly get the message that you have "left your receiver off the hook."

Honest listening means that you are willing to let your child say some things you would rather not hear. If your son tells you in confidence that his friend, your neighbor's son, is stealing money from his mother's purse, you have a problem you would rather not deal with. Are you going to tell your neighbor and risk losing a friend? On the other hand, if you can earn the trust of your child at an early age, so that he feels safe sharing his confidences, you will reap the benefits when the difficult years of adolescence come. It isn't enough, however, for your child to have faith in you. Somehow you must convey the idea that you have faith in him. Melissa, aged thirteen, shouted as her mother interrupted her,

"When I tell you about my problems, I don't want you to fix them. I just want you to listen!"

How can you expect your children to have confidence in themselves, unless they know you have confidence in them?

NO! NO! NO!

The development of language in the young child is one of life's marvels we take for granted. Between the time he speaks that first word and the age of five the average child will have acquired a large part of his basic vocabulary. His comprehension may take longer, as Gina's predicament made clear. The sensitive teacher or parent will be tuned in to the second language, behavior, which is often a child's only way of letting us know what he is feeling. Words for basic needs, "I want some milk," "Help me to put on my jacket," are learned easily. Words which say, "I'm scared," "I'm confused," "I'm angry!" "I'm jealous!" are hard for even grown-ups to express.

Teaching Comunication Skills

Oral communication is a skill, one which can be taught and which improves with practice. Even the tiny infant is absorbing words, storing them away in her brain where they can be retrieved later and put to use. In an infant center, staff are instructed to talk to the babies, explaining what they are doing. "I am going to wash you and put on a nice clean diaper," or naming objects, "This is a basket. It is filled with crackers." Even though one would have to question the degree of comprehension, this is "input," and when the programming is constant and consistent, the "output" will emerge at such an early age as to be astounding.

Language brings a sense of power to the toddler who discovers that the word "no" elicits a reaction. He uses it indiscriminately, often with little idea of its meaning, and the adult who tries to make something of it will be the loser — not necessarily at that moment, but in future situations. To make issues over prompt obedience at this stage is like trying to drive a car when the steering mechanism is broken — it can't function without the proper equipment. Marianna, a teacher who expected the children to do what she wanted them to, was a master at dealing with these little ones. "Oh yes, we will!" she would say with a smile, and taking the child by the hand, would proceed to follow through on her request. Recognizing his need to assert his independence, she wouldn't have dreamed of engaging in a confrontation with a child. This is in sharp contrast to a young father I witnessed recently who shouted, "No two year old is going to tell me...!"

There does come a time, usually at about age three, when the child understands the meaning of "no" but continues to test the limits of his power to resist. The burden is then on the adult to substitute positive statements for negative directions. "Walk in back of the swings!" or "Come this way" instead of "I told you not to run in front of the swings!" "Take another bite of your dinner" instead of "Stop messing around and clean up your plate!"

Many adults fail to realize how much their children can understand if given the chance.

"Talk-It-Over" Chairs

In one of the many child care centers I have visited, I met a teacher who had developed a method for helping children

solve their own "people" problems. It began one day when two little boys were fighting over a truck. Pulling two small chairs together she sat them down, facing each other, and with knees touching. "These are the 'talk-it-over' chairs," she said. "We are going to learn how to use words instead of fighting when we have a problem.

"Roberto, you punched Ivan because he tried to take the truck.

"Ivan, tell Roberto why you wanted the truck. No, Roberto, it's Ivan's turn to talk first. You will have a chance when he is through."

"He wasn't playing with it. He put it down, and I was waiting for it," Ivan said.

"But I wasn't through with it," Roberto sputtered. "I just left it a minute to go get the gas pump."

The conversation went back and forth, with the teacher standing by, interrupting only when she had to remind them to talk one at a time. They finally arrived at a compromise, and walked away to continue their play happily.

After the "talk-it-over" chairs had been used successfully several times, this teacher tried a second stage.

"Donna, you and Bonita seem to be having some difficulty," she said. "Why don't you try the 'talk-it-over' chairs?"

Solemnly, and with great dignity, Donna and Bonita carried out their own negotiations.

The real reward came on another day when two children, without any suggestion from this teacher, arranged the chairs, sat down, and carried through the "talk-it-over" process to a satisfactory conclusion.

Could some of these methods be applied in the home? With so many family members coming and going, each on a different schedule, communication requires a special effort but the pay-off is well worth it.

Pouring Fuel on the Flames

"Good morning, Tony," said the teacher with a warm smile, as the handsome, dark-eyed, four-year-old came into the nursery school. Instead of the cheerful response she expected, Tony brushed past her and went directly to the cubby area. In a moment there was a shriek of outrage.

"Tony knocked my coat down and put his jacket on my hook!"

"Tony!" exclaimed Fatima in surprise. "Why did you do that? You know which is your cubby. Here's your own picture on it."

The only answer was a defiant glare. For the next hour Tony moved through the classroom like a tornado, leaving anger and destruction in his wake.

"Tony scribbled on my picture!"

"Ms. Jacoby, make Tony get out of here! He knocked down our airport!"

"Tony hit me!"

"Tony took my baseball cap that my daddy gave me!"

With each episode, Fatima's patience grew thinner, her exasperation stronger, and her reprimands sharper. The last straw came when she saw Tony grab one corner of the cloth on a small table, sending the carefully-laid tea party to the floor.

"Tony, this is too much! I can't think what has gotten into you today. You have been naughty all morning. How can you expect to have any friends when you are so mean to them? Now you will have to come into my office and sit on a chair until you can behave."

Tony stared at her defiantly and did not budge. Rather

than drag him, Fatima picked up the rigid, resistant child and carried him into her office, where she sat him down, none too gently.

"I can't imagine what's wrong with you today, Tony," she said again. "I think I'll have to call your mother."

As if her words had opened a valve, the child burst into wild sobbing, and his rigid body crumpled,

Fatima's anger dissolved as she looked at him. "Oh, Tony," she said softly. "What is it, sweetheart? What has happened?" She picked him up gently, sat down in a big chair and held him close, making small, comforting sounds until his sobbing diminished. Again she asked, "What's wrong, Tony?"

He buried his head in her shoulder, and in muffled tones he said, "They took my mother away. She was all white. She had her eyes shut. They took her away in an ambulance."

"It's all right, dear. Everything is going to be all right," she said soothingly, as her mind raced with speculation. What had happened at Tony's house, and why in the world hadn't someone told her about it? And why, she thought, didn't I do some **INVESTIGATING**?

What had happened at Tony's house that morning? Tony's mother, three months pregnant, was awakened by sharp pains and found that she was bleeding profusely. Steve, her husband, called the doctor, who ordered an ambulance to get her to the hospital. Frantic with fear for his wife, Steve just barely had enough presence of mind to call his neighbor, Mrs. Anderson, and ask her to take care of Tony.

Tony came out into the hall in his pajamas in time to see two men carrying a thing that looked like a bed. His mother was on it, very pale, eyes closed. The men carried her down the stairs and out the front door. Tony began to tremble. Just then his father dashed out of his room, putting on his jacket as he came.

"Daddy," cried Tony. "Where are they taking Mummy?"

Barely pausing, his father answered quickly, "Mummy's sick. Mrs. Anderson will help you get dressed and get you ready for school. Be a good boy." As he rushed off, Tony ran to the window. The two men were closing the doors of the ambulance, and as it drove off the siren began to wail. Tony's stomach started churning, and he thought he was going to throw up.

Just then Mrs. Anderson came in and went into his room, pulling out drawers and looking for clothes. Hurriedly she dressed him, brushing aside his anxious questions. She hustled him across the street to her house, and gave him some breakfast, but he couldn't eat. His mind was whirling with questions. Where were they taking his mother? Why didn't Daddy take him, too? Why did his mother look so funny? Who were those men? Why was Mummy sick? What did that mean? Sick meant staying in bed and swallowing medicine, not being carried away, all white and still. Was she ever coming back?

He tried to ask Mrs. Anderson, but she kept saying, "I don't know. Hurry up, the school bus will be here any minute." Just then the school bus came and Mrs. Anderson rushed him out the door. She didn't kiss him goodbye, the way his mother always did.

Tony's small world had suddenly turned topsy-turvy, and he was scared. But as he went, his fear spilled over into anger, which exploded into action as soon as he went in the door.

There is a message in this story for both teachers and parents. Fatima Jacoby failed to apply two of the key steps in dealing with a child who is misbehaving, **HESITATE** and **INVESTIGATE**. Tony's behavior was contrary to his usual pattern, which should have caused her to **HESITATE**. If she had practiced the policy of "getting into the skin of the child" she would have said to herself, "Something must have happened to set off this unusual behavior. Until I get some clues, I will move with caution." Instead she reacted with anger and disapproval, thus pouring additional fuel on flames that were already burning in this troubled little boy.

As for **INVESTIGATING**, her first move should have been to call his home. In this case, since there was no one to answer, she would have turned to the emergency number listed, which might have been Mrs. Anderson's.

Most of all, this story points up the need to **COMMU-NICATE**. With the ambulance there and his wife on the way to the hospital, Steve should have taken time to ease Tony's mind. "Mummy is sick, and those men are taking her to the hospital where the doctor will take care of her. She's going to be all right, and in a few days she will be home. I can't take you with me because they don't let little boys in the hospital unless they are sick, but I will be here when you come home from school."

Likewise, in turning Tony over to Mrs. Anderson, he should have asked her to call the school and explain the situation.

Adults do not always think of the viewpoint of the child. We take their comprehension for granted. In any crisis, it is important to be sensitive to the concerns aroused in the child, and to explain the things that might be beyond his realm of experience. If this is not done, confusion and anger will manifest themselves in the only way he knows how to **COMMUNICATE** — through his behavior. How much less painful this whole situation would have been for Tony if the lines of communication had been open!

Communicating with adults is often difficult for young children because they have discovered that grown-ups can't be trusted but may punish them for telling the truth, or for explaining their feelings. Unfortunately, parents who test their children's love are not as uncommon as we might like to believe. An extreme example of the way a foolish parent destroyed her child's ability to trust follows.

CHAPTER 6

Basic Trust

With a strange choking sound, Mary Alice dropped to the floor and appeared to be unconscious.

"Mama! Mama!" screamed Audrey, her six-year-old daughter. "Are you sick? What is the matter? Please talk to me," she cried, patting her mother's cheek.

After what seemed an eternity to Audrey, her mother sat up, laughing, and said, "I'm all right. I just wanted to see how much you love me!"

As she related this story Audrey, now thirty years old and a mother herself, shuddered at the memory. "My mother was young and pretty," she said. "She loved it when people said we looked more like sisters than mother and daughter. But I didn't want to be her sister. She was my mother and I wanted her to be like the other kids' mothers. Everyone thought she was such a good mother. She kept my hair curled and dressed me in frilly dresses. I was really more like her doll than her child, and she treated me with the same inconsistency. One minute she was hugging and kissing me, and the next she turned away and ignored me. There were times she wouldn't speak to me for days and I never knew what I had done to offend her, but I was miserable because I was sure it had to be something bad. I carried a constant burden of guilt. It wasn't until I ended up on a psychiatrist's couch years later that I realized what she had done to me with her childish tricks. I couldn't trust anyone — the husband I loved, or my own children. That lack of trust has affected my whole life. I was always sure that someone was cheating me: the repairman had put someone else's worn tire on my car, the gas station attendant charged me the wrong price, the storekeeper had his thumb on the scales. The only way I can bear to maintain a relationship with my mother now is to try to feel sorry for her," Audrey continued sadly. "She is still wrapped up in herself and I'm sure she has no idea what she did to me!"

Trust is the Core of Relationships

Basic trust begins at the moment of birth when the infant emerges from the protected warm environment of the womb into a cold, harsh world where his senses are assaulted with light and noise. If he is treated with loving care, fed when he is hungry, changed when he is wet and uncomfortable, cuddled and comforted, he comes to know the world as a good place, and his beginning self-concept is founded on security and trust.

But what if he is neglected? Fed only after he cries himself purple? Left sodden in his crib for hours? What if his most important needs for nurturing contact and being held are ignored? What will his impressions be then?

The seeds of insecurity which Mary Alice planted in her little daughter's developing "self" grew into an ugly weed of distrust, which affected her relationships with people throughout her life.

Parents Are Not Always Perfect

However, there is such a thing as letting the pendulum swing too far the other way. In your efforts to do what is best for your child, there will be failures. You must not let yourself be eaten up with guilt if you lose your temper or if you say the wrong thing or in any way betray your own goals. We aren't perfect. We do the best we can.

In Audrey's case, her ability to cope with her mother's foolishness was hampered by the image presented to the outside world of a loving, caring relationship. Each time she heard her mother receive compliments for being such a *good* mother it reinforced her belief that she must be a *bad* child.

Child Abuse Isn't Always Physical

The immature behavior exhibited by Mary Alice in this story leaves us with feelings of shock and disgust. This was a clear case of abuse, but because there were no visible signs of physical harm, it went undetected. Child abuse has been brought into the public view in recent years and legislation requiring an observer to report it, or be subject to a fine, is a step in the right direction. The kind of emotional abuse Mary Alice inflicted on Audrey is more subtle, and less likely to be observed than black and blue marks and cigarette burns, but the ill effects are just as serious, and may even be more lasting.

Love, Respect and Consistency

How then do we instill a feeling of trust in our children? The first key is love — steady, unqualified, undemanding **LOVE**; love which offers security and protection but is able to let go when the fledgling is ready to fly; love which allows liberty but will not tolerate license. A parent may say, "I do not like that thing you are doing, but I will never stop loving you."

The second element is **RESPECT**. Some parents treat their children as if they were toys — inanimate objects put on this earth for their amusement or to do their bidding. These parents talk about their good and bad features in their presence, acting as if they were not persons who can hear.

"Charles isn't a bit like his brother, William," Mrs. Whalen told his teacher on his first day in school.

Hearing his mother say it just confirmed his own opinion that he was dumb.

Parents embarrass and humiliate their children before others, criticizing their appearance, behavior, or attempts to be like adults.

"Go wash that filthy face!" Mother says to Freida as she comes running in from her play to greet her visiting grandmother. "Nana doesn't want to kiss a dirty face!"

"Hey Dummy! You've got your pants on backwards," Dad says to Karl. "Get back in your room and change them!" when he could have ignored the mistake and congratulated his son for dressing himself.

And parents aren't the only ones guilty of such rude behavior.

"Not very P-R-E-T-T-Y," one visitor spelled out to another.

"No, but very S-M-A-R-T!" five-year-old Deborah interjected with a gleeful look in her eye.

There is a simple basic rule which, if followed by parents, would prevent a lot of problems: Treat your child with the same courtesy you would accord a guest in your home.

And so we build our trust relationship on **LOVE** and **RESPECT**. The third ingredient is **CONSISTENCY**. The parent who is indulgent and amused by a particular bit of behavior one day, but reacts with screaming and punishment when the pattern is repeated on another occasion, leaves the child in a state of confusion. He wants to please the adult who holds the key to his security. He needs to feel the approval of that person, but how can he know what will win it for him when the rules change every day?

It is hard to be consistent. Adults who have problems with discipline may never have faced up to their own feelings. They are afraid to admit to their own hostility, and since punishment is, at least in their view, an act of aggression, they are unable to take a firm stand. Furthermore, adults themselves are subject to mood changes. When everything is going smoothly it is easy to be patient, reasonable and understanding, but in the pressurized world we confront today that state of euphoria seldom exists for long. The working parent who comes home at the end of a stressful day, accompanied by a whining, fretful child, has to dig deep in her well of inner reserves to behave with consistency, love and respect.

What is the key to this all-important consistency? How does a parent go about achieving it?

Set the ground rules. In your own mind, decide what standards of behavior are important, and how you can enforce them.

For example, if you do not want your children to be rude or to "talk back" to adults, make up your mind that you will never laugh at such behavior or treat it lightly.

Guidelines for behavior must be agreed upon in advance by the whole family. When this harmony is lacking, a bright child will quickly grasp the opportunity to play one parent against the other.

CHAPTER 7

Parents Are Teachers

I'll Teach You!

"Bus 135, N.Y. to Boston, leaving from Station 6!"

When the announcement came over the speaker, Zelda wearily picked up her suitcase and grasped two-year-old Molly by the hand. Her six-year-old son was carrying a shopping bag bulging with sweaters, coloring books and crayons, small cars, and other paraphernalia while his sister struggled with a stuffed rabbit which was her equal in size.

"Go on, Sam," Zelda urged, prodding him from behind. "Hurry up. People are waiting to get on."

"I want to sit by the window," Molly whined, as Sam hustled into that favored spot.

"No way!" he grinned. "I got here first!"

Molly set up a howl and Zelda sat down and pulled her onto her lap. "Shhh!" she said, soothingly. "You will have a turn later. We have a long time to be on this bus."

As they left the city the children were busy looking out the window. When they began to get restless, Zelda brought forth the coloring books and settled down to read a magazine, hoping for a breather — but it was not to be.

"I have to pee," Sam announced in a loud voice.

"Me, too!" Molly was quick to follow.

"You just went in the bus station," Zelda whispered. "It's too soon to go again."

"But I have to!" Sam wailed, jumping up and down. "I'm going to wet my pants!"

Zelda, her face flushed with embarrassment, started down the aisle to the lavatory at the rear of the bus, pushing Sam ahead of her again and carrying Molly. The children beamed and smiled at the passengers, obviously ready to respond to any friendly overture.

When they were back in their seats, Zelda tried once more to read. Molly had the window seat this time. For a few minutes all was quiet, and then the argument began again.

"Molly's had the window for a long time! It's my turn now!"

"It is not! You had it longer!"

"Here, Sam, why don't you read this book to Molly?" Zelda said, as she handed him a story book.

"No, I don't wanna," Sam answered, sulkily.

"Yes you do. I wanna hear it," Molly whined, whereupon Sam used the book to whack Molly on the head.

Her frustration blew the lid right off Zelda's patience. "I'll teach you to hit people," she screamed, as she slapped Sam in the face!

AND SHE DID!

How does this story make you feel? Does Zelda's lack of control shock you? Does it dredge up guilty memories of times when you have shown a similar display of temper?

I first heard the story when I was attending a lecture given by Dr. Lawrence Frank, a well-known educator.

Those words, "I'll teach you to hit people!" were indelibly etched on my mind and from that day have flashed warning signals when I have been on the verge of teaching the wrong behavior through my own actions. At such times I can see Dr. Frank standing there on the stage, his kindly face topped with a shock of white hair, and I hear him say, in a dramatically quiet tone,

"And she did!"

How often do we as parents and teachers teach our children to do the very things we punish them for? We yell or shout at them in angry tones and then we scold them for engaging in shouting matches with their peers. We criticize them, embarrass and humiliate them in front of others as if they were robots instead of feeling, human beings but we are outraged when they indulge in name calling, hurt their friends with such labels as "Fatso" or "Dummy," or resort to racial slurs.

With the best intentions we allow ourselves to attack children verbally — and even physically — when, if we could all have a warning signal which flashes automatically, it might serve as a brake when our emotions take precedence over reason.

No Cookbook Recipes

In our frustration we are all reaching for clearly defined answers. There are "how to" books on every conceivable subject. A publisher once told me that the two most popular are cookbooks and books on discipline, and it occurred to me that if someone were clever enough to combine the two subjects, it might turn out to be a best seller! If I want to make an apple dumpling I can go to my favorite cookbook and find a recipe. Parents would love to be able to thumb through the index of a book and find a sure-fire recipe for dealing with fighting, lying, or temper tantrums. Teachers and parents would be grateful for tried and true formulas that would enable them to control unruly children!

Unfortunately, there can never be cookbook recipes for dealing with human behavior because the ingredients will never be the same in any two situations. Each incident will be the result of a combination of people with unique personalities, the environment in which it takes place, and the immediate circumstances. These ingredients are stable but they will never be measured out in the same amounts and so the product is unpredictable. The thread of consistency which can weave them together is the definition we have chosen. If our goal is clear and if the ultimate result we seek is a child who has learned self-discipline, we will not turn out look-alike people but we will find joy and satisfaction in the process of developing confident, competent individuals.

Halos of Heroes

There is one thing parents and teachers have in common, which is also their greatest asset. Whether they deserve it or not, whether they like it or not, they wear the halos of heroes. Every child really wants to bask in the sunshine of the approval of a favored adult. At home, it is one or both parents; in school, it is the teacher.

The word "discipline" stems from "disciple" and a disciple is one who identifies with his leader, and who consciously tries to follow in his footsteps. The leaders in a child's world are his parents and his teachers. A child needs to look up to his parents, for they represent his only security in a world which can be very frightening. We hear the little boy boasting, "My father is BIG!" "My father is strong — he can fight anyone!" "My father is so smart — he knows!" and even though his father may look ordinary, he is a hero in his child's eyes.

On the other hand, we have only to observe children playing "school" to recognize that they copy their teacher's mannerisms and tone of voice.

Living up to such admiration places an awesome responsibility on all of us, but at the same time it gives us an advantage. If we can believe that deep in his heart the child wants to please us, we may be able to transcend our immediate reaction when we are on the receiving end of a well-placed kick in the shins or a torrent of four-letter words. We may even act like mature adults instead of unequally matched antagonists. If we can rise to a level where we are asking, "What can be going on in the life of this child which makes him want to lash out at the world?" we can look for reasons behind the behavior. At that point we will be on our way toward making the definition work.

CHAPTER 8

Doing What Comes Naturally

Up to this point we have been talking about disciplinary situations which had dramatic beginnings, when in fact most of our troubles revolve around the simple, necessary routines of daily living. Eating, eliminating, and sleeping are natural processes, but it is easy to let these routine procedures develop into headlock confrontations.

"The child care center won't accept my child if she isn't toilet trained," the frustrated mother agonizes.

"I'm supposed to give my child a nutritionally balanced diet, but no one tells me what to do when he won't even taste vegetables!"

Instead of letting simple, necessary routines become problems, we might well listen to the advice of this experienced teacher in a child care center.

"Louise, how does it happen that when you eat with the children everyone is so quiet and peaceful? They never throw food around or leave a big mess under the table."

"Yes, and I don't hear the kids at your table saying 'Yuk! I hate this stuff!' the way some of mine do," another teacher chimed in. "It only takes one, and my whole group decides not to eat. I think Lenny just does it to bug me!"

"And how is it that when you are in charge of the nap room everyone goes to sleep?" another teacher inquired. "They just seem to be waiting for me. No one sleeps. One starts jumping on his cot and then another and the more I scold the worse they get. Just when I think I have them all settled down someone has to go to the bathroom and that starts another round. By the time they all settle down — if they do — I am the one who needs the nap!"

Louise, a woman in her fifties with an ample bosom and a readily available lap, looked up in surprise. "Well," she answered slowly and thoughtfully, "I guess they just know I like them, and they want to please me. I sort of expect that they will do what I ask them to, and they do it!"

It sounded much too simple, but Louise was right. Young children are quick to sense it when an adult is apprehensive. When they discover that negative behavior can arouse anxiety in a teacher, they make the most of it. But actually, down deep, most children do not really want it that way. It makes them uneasy when an adult abdicates the position of authority. Children need to be able to press against the security of boundaries, and know that they will remain firm. "I know my mother (teacher) will not let me" feels better than a shaky, "Who will stop me if I go too far?"

Eating in the Home

Trouble in the home often starts with an over-anxious mother.

"Eat your vegetables!" she says. "They are good for you!" And when Ahmed says, "No, I hate vegetables!" she lets a simple situation build up into a battle of wills.

"I'm not going to eat that icky stuff," Tana whines, pushing back her plate petulantly. "You know I hate spaghetti. Why did you give it to me?"

Instead of a calm response such as, "That is what we are having today. If you don't want to eat it, you can have bread and butter," this mother offers, "How would you like a nice poached egg on toast?" and lets her own meal get cold while she hurries to prepare it.

"Clean up everything on that plate or you can't have any dessert," Dad orders.

"If you don't at least taste the broccoli, there will be no television for you tonight!" Mom threatens.

Eating should be taken for granted. Threats, bribes and rewards attach undue importance to an act which should be as matter-of-fact as breathing. If you issue a threat, you must expect your bright, intelligent child to accept the challenge. Suddenly you find yourself in a headlock, a situation in which someone will have to back down.

Does any of this strike a familiar note? If you have been trapped into a battle of wills over eating, how can you extricate yourself?

First, stop worrying. A normal, healthy child will not starve if he misses a meal. In fact, when the attention ceases to focus on him he will probably eat what you put before him. He may not eat as much as you think he should, and he may not choose to eat in the order you suggest, but he will eat when he is hungry.

A Touch of Class

The second bit of advice is to create an environment which is conducive to gracious living if you want your child to acquire social skills. When my children were young, I discovered that when we ate in the kitchen, I was continually nagging.

"Stop tipping your chair back!"

"Ask your sister to pass the butter. You don't have to reach across the table."

"Don't try to talk with your mouth full!"

But when we ate in the dining room by candlelight and on the best dishes, my offspring rose to the occasion. An attractive setting seemed to lead automatically to better manners and good conversation. It even worked on me! I tended to give more thought to the way I prepared and served the food. That is probably when I learned what I so often preach, "If you treat your children with the same courtesy that you give a guest in your home, many of your behavioral conflicts will just melt away." We all like to be proud of our children when we take them out to eat, either in a restaurant or a friend's home. Somewhere they have to learn the skills and home should be the training ground!

When I talk with my grown-up children about what they remember of their early years, they will often say, "The times we sat around the table after dinner, just talking." It was a time for sharing, for easy conversation. (When I was a child, adults talked and children waited until they were invited to speak.)

There should be some rules established which will make mealtime pleasurable. It should be agreed that squabbling and arguing cannot be tolerated at the table. Dinner time should never be used to play back the day's mistakes and misdemeanors. Subjects which stir the emotions, and interfere with digestion, such as Victor's report card, whether Felicia is going out after dinner, or why Hank can't have sixty dollars for a new electronic game, should be reserved for a more appropriate time and place. It is pretty hard to enjoy food when your stomach is knotted with anxiety or resentment!

Table Manners

"But if I don't call attention to table manners how can I expect my children to learn?" an anxious parent may be wondering.

By setting a good example. Imagine that you are at a dinner party. If a fellow guest slurped his soup, or ate his peas with a knife, you would not criticize him in front of other guests. Your children are entitled to the same consideration. Mention an error later, in a casual way, when you are alone. Praise him quietly when you see that he has made a conscious effort to improve.

Eating in the Child Care Center

The main responsibility for the upbringing of the child rests with the parents but the reality is that more than half of our children are spending eight to ten hours a day in care outside the home. This means that a caregiver is the role model. When I visit a child care center, one of the criteria I use for determining quality care is the manner in which the meal is conducted. I look for programs which make a real effort to duplicate the environment of a good home.

If I see teachers standing around eating off their plates, chatting with each other while the children are noisy, grabbing, standing up and reaching to get what they want, it is not a model of a good mealtime.

In a well run center I saw children helping to set the table. One child was chosen to go to the kitchen for the food. One adult sat at each table and served the food. (The director explained that when two adults were at a table, they were inclined to talk to each other, excluding the children. One of the goals at mealtime was to encourage conversation, with every child participating.)

A set of rules had been drawn up with the help of the children and posted on the wall near the table. Thus the teacher could say "Look at number 7, Lars," instead of "How many times do I have to tell you not to stuff so much into your mouth at one time?"

The teacher made one thing clear at the outset. "If you do not like what we are having to eat you will not talk about it. You may think about it, but we do not wish to hear it. Tell us if something looks or tastes good, or better still, tell Mrs. Carle (the cook). It will make her happy."

You Can't Win!

To conclude the subject of eating, there is one thought that seldom occurs to the adult. In most of life's situations the child is at your mercy. He must conform because you are bigger and stronger. When it comes to eating, he holds the trump card. You may be able to force a child to eat, you can hold his nose

so he has to swallow what's in his mouth, but you cannot make him retain it. Push him too far and he will manage to bring it back up!

Eliminating

The same principle applies to toilet training, another function in which the child holds the power. I get a desperate letter every so often from some poor teacher or director who pleads, "What can we do with the four-year-old who messes his pants day after day? We make him sit on the toilet until he has ridges on his butt with no results, and five minutes later he will deliberately soil himself. Why would an apparently normal child do this?"

Toddlers will have accidents, and two's and three's may occasionally be too preoccupied with playing or wait too long before going to the toilet, but when a child of four or older has innumerable accidents it is time to **INVESTIGATE**. The parents, teachers, and perhaps an outside professional, need to work as a team to discover the underlying cause.

Parents should call the pediatrician. It is possible that the muscles that control that function are not fully developed.

Occasionally, a child can become so absorbed in doing something he likes that he ignores the growing urgency to eliminate.

Consider whether your child is going to extraordinary measures to gain more of your attention. We know that children will deliberately disobey the rules and accept punishment if that is the only way they can get their favorite adult's attention. Even though you may sputter and scold while you clean him up, he may enjoy just standing there and letting you.

The parent of a first child may have unwittingly caused the problem by making a big issue of it the first time it happened. If she has been advised that a child should be toilet trained at a certain age, she may have started to worry when it didn't happen on the right day of the right month of the right year. It can even become a matter of pride. She may see it as a reflection on her own mothering skills.

If Ann Jonas proudly boasts that her son was fully trained at the age of eighteen months, Elisa Crews may exert pressure on her baby to measure up to the same standard, without realizing that his sphincter muscles are not yet fully developed. Each child is unique, and her rate of progress must be respected. Your child can "read" your anxiety long before she can read from a book.

"My grandson, Ricci, is a very bright five-year-old," Gretchen confided in me hesitantly, "but he has a real problem, and it's driving my daughter crazy. At least three times a week he will mess his pants. She has tried scolding and punishing, but nothing seems to work. He just stands there and lets her clean up that horrible stinky mess!"

"Tell her to take him into the bathroom and explain that the next time he will have to take care of it himself. As casually as she would teach him the proper way to wash his hands, she should talk him through the clean-up process, step by step. The next time it happens she should hand him a set of clean clothes and say, 'Go into the bathroom and get cleaned up. Remember, I showed you how.' Then walk away. He may not do a great job the first time, but if she is matter-of-fact about it he will get the message."

Gretchen called me a week later. "It worked!" she said. "Ricci had to try it twice to be sure his mother meant it, and then it stopped. He hasn't done it since."

"That's great," I replied. "Now tell her about positive reinforcement. When they are alone, she can praise him, let him know that she is proud of him."

If this solution doesn't work, and no physical cause is found, punishment with fair warning may be necessary. The important point is to choose a punishment which fits the crime.

"I'm afraid you can't go to the park with Sarah and me. There is no bathroom there to change messy pants."

"Yes, that's the ice cream truck, but you wouldn't want to go out there with those smelly pants."

How can a teacher handle this problem in group care? Many centers will not accept a child until she is toilet-trained, but when it is esssential for a parent to work, it isn't easy to make that a requirement for admission.

I suggest that centers request that children who are ready to be trained wear training pants, not diapers. The first few times a child messes his pants the teacher should clean her, giving her time to adjust to the new situation. After a few days, she should hand the child clean clothes and send her to the toilet to change, just as the mother did in the previous story. Cleanup in the center should include putting the soiled clothing into a bag to be carried home.

Success, whether in the home or at school, depends on the adult's ability to be matter-of-fact. When a child senses that she is engaged in a battle of wills, she may prolong the process.

Occasionally the problem is reversed; a child may withhold his bowel movements. The cause may be physical or psychological but in either case it is a warning sign of a problem which should not be ignored.

Sleeping

Bedtime often becomes the battleground for clashing wills. The key is consistency. It helps to state the rules on paper, leaving no ground for argument. A sample might be:

Bedtime is seven-thirty.
Starting at seven o'clock

1. Get undressed
2. Go to the bathroom
3. Wash hands
4. Brush teeth
5. Say good night to the family
6. Get into bed where you may:
   Have a story read to you,
   or listen to one record,
   or look at books.
7. At seven-thirty the light will be put out.

To avoid the issue of "one more drink of water" place a glass of water on the table beside the child's bed. Do not respond to conversation once she is in bed. It can go on for as long as you are willing to prolong it.

There will be arguments: "Why do I have to go to bed at seven-thirty if Isaac can stay up until eight?"

"I'm not tired!"

"If I promise to go to bed very fast, can I stay up just this once to watch this program?"

Alyson was five when she said at the supper table, "Can I go to bed as early as I want to tonight?" Her astonished parents looked at her. Was this the little girl who was always teasing to stay up a little longer?

"Sure you can," said her father.

"Good! Then I'll go to bed at midnight. That's as early as I want."

Caught, her parents agreed, but nature intervened, and at nine-thirty a heavy-eyed Alyson gave up and chose to go to bed.

Sometimes the problem isn't just getting the child to bed but in keeping him there. It may start when he is frightened by a nightmare or sudden storm. He awakens a sleepy mother who takes the easy way out and lets him crawl in beside her. It's all cozy and warm, much nicer than being in a separate room all alone. Hard as it is at the time, a parent should get out of bed and put the child back in his own bed, staying a while if necessary to comfort him. The end result will be best for all concerned.

Some children get out of bed and wander through the house while their parents are sleeping, a dangerous habit. There is no easy solution. You must not lock his bedroom door! Offer as many compromises as you can, such as, "You may turn on your light and play as long as you stay in your own room and are quiet."

Buy a lunch box and pack a little snack. Let him listen to a tape.

Adults should use a reasonable degree of understanding of special situations or circumstances, but variations ought to be rare. If rules change frequently they lose significance. It then becomes a matter of who can win the debate.

Children need to know that it is the adult who makes the decisions. I have seen parents let their children rationalize, argue, and explain and reason ad infinitum, when they should have said, "This is the way it is — period."

These three functions, eating, sleeping and eliminating, are necessary for survival. Society imposes additional skills which can bring on another whole set of behavior problems. Children have to learn to clothe their bodies and keep them clean. We live in such a hurried, busy world that parents are tempted to do for the child what he can learn to do for himself.

Dressing and Washing

"Here, let me do it!" Mother says in an exasperated tone as she tugs on boots. "I haven't got all day to wait for you!"

"No, I can't wait for you to dress yourself. I'll be late for work!" as she hustles her daughter into her clothes.

In the preschool or child care center, there should always be TIME. Teachers can slowly and patiently teach children the HOW, and give them ample time to do it themselves. Learning to button, zip, tie and lace are part of the education process, and the child's I AM grows with each small success.

The reverse problem is occasionally one of getting a child to keep his clothes on. A teacher in a child care center related an amusing situation. Emil insisted on taking his shoes off and walking around the classroom in his bare feet. His teacher had tried being patient, stern, cross and punishing — all with no success. One day Emil came to her.

"I'll make you a proposition!" he said.

Wondering where a four-year-old might have heard those words, she answered, "O.K. What is it?"

"I'll keep my shoes on if you will let me move the toy sink."

"Sure, where do you want to put it?" she queried.

"Over here, so I can look out the window when I 'wash' the dishes," was the answer. And holding true to his word, he did keep his shoes on after that.

Teaching a child how to wash and dry his hands and face, how to brush his teeth and take care of his toileting are all a legitimate part of the preschool program. Remembering their own schooling, caregivers are inclined to think "curriculum" relates only to intellectual activities, when actually, skills for daily living are the foundation which makes later learning possible.

There is one thing parents can do which will save wear and tear on them and encourage the child. They can look at the **ENVIRONMENT**, and the way it prevents children from doing the very things we demand of them. The mother who sends her child back to wash his face again might have saved that irritation if she had placed a mirror at his eye level.

When a full length mirror is easily accessible a child can be taught to look at her appearance, and possibly discover that her socks don't match or her shirt is dirty.

If each of us had to spend one whole day in a house which was built for giants, with tables, chairs, beds and toilets which were proportionally as outsized as the furniture we expect our children to use, we might be more understanding of their problems. We can put a small stool in the bathroom, which can be used in front of the toilet and washbowl. We can hang a towel rack where little hands can reach it. Going back to the analogy of the guest, we know that a considerate hostess anticipates the needs of guests and tries to make them comfortable. Can we do less for our children?

A Sense of Order

Before we leave the subject of **ENVIRONMENT**, let's take a look at the demands we make on children to maintain a neat appearance, and to keep their belongings in order. How much help do we give them? One facet of Montessori training with which I wholeheartedly agree is the emphasis on a child's need for order. From his earliest days if there is "a place for everything" and he is expected to put things back in that place when he is finished with them, a basic training process is set in motion which will pay dividends. Ordering objects is a foundation for reading and math. Ordering thought processes is essential to formal education. It begins with the ability to *see the sense* in putting things where they belong.

It is nice if children can learn to put their underwear, socks and shirts neatly in bureau drawers, but three shoe boxes, decorated and marked, can serve the same purpose.

Speaking of boxes and order, I can't miss an opportunity to speak of my pet peeve — the traditional toy chest. It may be very attractive on the outside, but it teaches all the wrong things. When mother stands at the door of a room and says, "Clean up this mess right now!" what does the child do? Scoops everything up and throws it into the box. The room may look better, but how can we berate her for being destructive when we teach her to throw small cars, puzzle pieces, coloring books, broken crayons and torn books all into one giant heap? The toy chest is the ultimate example of adult inconsistency!

What is a better way? Provide low shelves. Draw pictures to fit each object to show where it belongs. Again the shoe boxes can be utilized to store small toys. In a good child care center the children are taught how to take care of the materials. When they are allowed to be careless with their own things at home, we teach them the wrong lessons.

CHAPTER 9

Behavior That Bugs You

The problems discussed in the previous chapter are all the results of over-zealous attempts to "train" children to do what should come naturally. We often act like a gardener who can't wait for nature to produce the blossoms and tries to pick and pull blooms out of buds. Small children offer us a never ending lesson in patience. The tussles we get into over these basic performances are only the beginning — the forerunner of more serious behavior which most children will exhibit at one time or another. The relationship we establish in these first encounters will work for, or against, us when we have to deal with lying, pilfering, squabbling, biting and other acts of aggression. Looking at her innocent beautiful baby, it is hard for a mother to imagine that she will ever have to deal with such transgressions, but to be forewarned is to be forearmed.

Biting

At some point before your child reaches the age of six he is likely to bite another human being. When it happens, if you remember what you are reading here, you may be able to take it in your stride. If you express horror, shock or anger; if you shout, shake or punish your child severely, you may create a mountain out of a molehill. On the other hand, if you can say to yourself, "Well, she said it would happen and here it is. Now what do I do?" you will be able to devote your energy to

corrective treatment. Certainly I am not suggesting that you should ignore it when your child bites, or treat it lightly. You must impress on the child that this is something you will not tolerate.

Of all the behavioral problems the parents or teachers of a preschool child may encounter, probably biting invokes the strongest feelings. Everyone's personality, pride and defense mechanisms are drawn into the maelstrom of emotions.

If we can accept the fact that biting is common with young children, we can then ask ourselves what we can do about it.

First, consider the age of the child. The infant bites because his gums hurt, and to bite down hard on something gives relief. Whether the object he bites is inanimate or alive is not part of his concern.

With toddlers and two's, it may be just a social advance. At this early age little children are as quick to express their desire to make friends with a push, shove, slap, or squeeze as they are with a pat or a kiss.

When a four- or five-year-old bites it is most important to look for the cause. This is the manifestation of a deeper problem. Something is going on in this child's life which is disturbing him enough to get his world "out of synch," and his behavior is a means for expressing his anxiety.

When a child bites repeatedly in group care, the director should ask the parents to come in for a conference. Together, director, teacher and parents will try to find the underlying cause for this behavior. Is something going on at home, or in school, that has thrown this child off balance?

Parents should try not to take it personally if the director suggests that the child should stay at home for a few days. Remember, she has to consider the other children and the angry parents of the child who has been bitten. What often happens is that if a parent can arrange to give the child more attention for a few days, the situation resolves itself. Or, if the child realizes that he is staying home because of the biting, and he misses his friends at school, he may exert the necessary self-control.

Young children are not able to put themselves in another's place. They have no sense of inflicting hurt. At the time of the incident, the teacher has to deal with her own emotions of anger and concern, and with the feelings of both the children involved.

The child who was bitten should have immediate comfort and care. After treating the injury, the teacher might give him some ice cubes wrapped in a paper towel to hold against it. Then something must be done about the offender.

It is better to get down to his level where you can look right in his eyes, hold him firmly and talk about it. Do not go into a verbal tirade about his being naughty or bad, or tell him he will not have any friends. This is a waste of your emotional energy and it usually falls on deaf ears. Do say, "It hurt Stavros when you bit him. See, your teeth made a mark on his arm. Teeth are for eating food, but you MAY NOT BITE PEOPLE!"

You may remove him from the group temporarily, but not in a way which humiliates him or embarrasses him. It is important that the biter doesn't win. Don't let him have the toy they were fighting over.

Sometimes it works to place a toddler in a play pen, explaining that, "You will have to play by yourself for a while because you hurt Stavros."

When all else fails, and if you absolutely must keep the child in the group, the only safe, effective method is to have one adult within arm's reach every minute of the day, ready to anticipate the act and move fast. It need not be the same person. Different staff members can be assigned fifteen minute periods of "guard duty," but you do have an obligation to protect the other children.

This is probably one of the most difficult problems to resolve in the entire scope of child care. Very little has been written about it because the "experts" are reluctant to offer pat answers. Indeed there are none, since everything depends on the circumstances. However, there is one point on which I believe there would be general agreement. You never, never try to "teach" the child by biting him to show him that it hurts. Children look up to grown-ups who are caring for them. If an adult bites, the message conveyed is that this is acceptable behavior. Such a simplified attack on the problem is really a cop-out, a sign that the parent or teacher is not willing to expend the time or energy to help children *see the sense in acting in a certain way.*

Lying

Let me state unequivocally that I do not believe that children under the age of four lie or steal. They may make statements which, by adult standards, are untrue, and they pick up whatever attracts them because they have not reached the age when there is a sharp distinction between "yours" and "mine." They cannot deal with this as "right" or "wrong." It would be hard to say when this awareness occurs. Maturity cannot be measured in exact time spans, but it is better to give children the benefit of the doubt than to accuse them unjustly. This was demonstrated in the following incidents.

"Oh, Ms. Kiuchi!" Mrs. Foster wailed over the phone. "What am I going to do with Leslie? She tells such awful lies. I have tried to tell her it is wicked but she doesn't listen to me!"

Leslie was Mrs. Foster's only child, born when her parents were past the usual child bearing age, and these calls were an almost daily occurrence, so with a resigned shrug of her shoulders Ms. Kiuchi asked, "What kind of stories does she tell?"

"Well," Leslie's mother responded indignantly, "yesterday when we were having lunch she told me this crazy story about the pony eating his cart. When I tried to tell her I knew it was a make-believe story she insisted that it was true! I'm sure I ought to curb this right now, but I don't know what to do. I hate to punish her."

"Would it surprise you to know," Ms. Kiuchi responded with a laugh, "that she was telling the truth? You may not have noticed it but Queenie's stable is divided. She stands on one side and the basket cart is on the other. Yesterday she did reach over and take a bite out of the rim. It was the main topic of conversation for the whole day. Of course Leslie wanted to tell you about it!"

Young children, especially before they have developed a conscience, which occurs sometime around the age of five, are also in the process of developing an imagination. Language is a newly discovered tool with which they enjoy experimenting. Some of their stories are pure fantasy, and should be treated as such, but parents must be careful not to jump to that conclusion, as is plain in the next incident.

Truth is Stranger Than Fiction

Virginia's mother was trying very hard to be a good parent. She read all of the books and magazine articles, and called upon Kristen, the nursery school director, frequently, for advice. One day after dropping off her child, she stopped in with a complaint.

"I'm really worried about Virginia," she began. "Lately she has been telling me the wildest stories. I know what you have said about children's imaginations, but what should I do when I know it must be a lie? If I pretend to believe it, won't I be teaching her that lying is acceptable?"

"What is her latest story?" Kristen asked. "Perhaps we can figure out what you should have said."

"It was really kind of gruesome," Virginia's mother said, with a shudder. "All about making snakes, and putting them on a stick, and cooking them over a fire, and eating them! How can she dream up such ridiculous tales?"

"Did you ever go to camp when you were a child?" Kristen asked.

"No, but what has that to do with Virginia's lying?" her mother replied with an annoyed expression.

"Well, it happens that Margherita, Virginia's teacher, worked in a day camp last summer and learned how to make bread twists. She asked me if she could try it with her children, and apparently it was successful."

"What is a bread twist?" Mrs. Taylor asked, thinking she was being put off.

"Well, first they mixed up a batch of good stiff biscuit dough. The children were able to help with that. Then Margherita gave each of the children a piece of dough and showed them how to roll it between their hands to make a 'snake', just as they do when they play with clay. Then they wrapped it round and round a stick and held it over a charcoal fire, turning it slowly. When it was puffed up and golden brown, she helped them slip it off carefully. Next they dropped a piece of butter and some jelly down the coiled bread and they ate them. They were delicious! Why don't you come over some day and they can do it again."

These two amusing anecdotes stress the fact that the truth *is* sometimes stranger than fiction, and adults should **INVESTIGATE** before making accusations or punishing a child without further inquiry.

It does no great harm to play along for a bit with comments such as, "Oh, that is very interesting. Tell me more about it." But when it is obvious that the story is a fantasy, it is also important to make that distinction with the child. You certainly do not punish him for it. Fantasy is not lying. It is creative story telling. What, then, is lying?

Why Do They Tell Lies?

When a person, child or adult, consciously and deliberately changes the truth in order to avoid punishment, to win unearned praise, to get someone else into trouble or to gain attention — that is lying. When this behavior becomes a habit, serious trouble is looming ahead.

You teach by example. Parents are the child's first and most consistent teachers. Teachers and preachers come and go, and have varying influences on their subjects, but parents are there year after year. As they struggle through each of the developmental stages, hoping that the next one will be easier, they can never lose sight of the inescapable fact that they provide the role models after which a child will pattern his personality and character. If he hears and sees his parents twisting the truth to serve their own ends, what will he learn?

Joan hears her mother call her father's office to say he is sick, when Joan knows he is going to the ball game.

"That dented fender happened in another accident, but put it down," Hans hears his father tell the insurance adjuster as he slips him some money. "I might as well collect on it while I have the chance. I pay big enough premiums!"

"I'm so sorry, I won't be able to take my turn helping at the church thrift shop tomorrow," Mrs. Hinds says on the phone. "I have just heard that I have company coming."

"Who's coming, Mother?" Kinesha asks with excited anticipation.

"No one," her mother replies, exasperated at being overheard. "I want to go in town tomorrow to have lunch with my friends. I might even get that new doll you have been wanting — so you didn't hear me make that phone call," she finishes with a conspiratorial smile.

What does twelve-year-old Christian learn when he hears

his mother tell the ticket seller at the movie, "He's only eleven. He's tall for his age."

Sometimes we make it almost impossible for a child to tell the truth.

Flora gasped in dismay when she entered the living room and saw her favorite vase in pieces on the floor in a puddle of water and scattered flowers. In one corner of the room was Georgie's large red ball. "Georgie!" yelled Flora.

The kitchen door opened, and slowly the five-year-old entered, his eyes avoiding the broken vase.

Her eyes snapping with anger, and in a voice shaking with fury, Flora shouted, "That is the vase Aunt Joanna gave me. It is a very valuable vase. Did you or didn't you break it?"

What is Georgie going to do? He doesn't have to be told that if he admits to breaking the vase, punishment is going to be swift and painful. If he thinks there is any chance of blaming the catastrophe on the cat, his baby sister, or a rush of wind, he is going to do it.

What, then, could Flora do instead? She doesn't have to disguise the fact that she is upset, and she does have to find out if Georgie really was responsible, but hopefully with some self-control, in a voice more troubled than enraged. This greatly increases the chances of Georgie's telling the truth. Then comes the tricky part. It is important to acknowledge that telling the truth is hard. Suppose Flora were to say, "Thank you. I know it wasn't easy to tell me that. I'm proud of you for telling the truth. Nevertheless, you did break the rule about playing ball in the living room, and the vase got broken. I have to punish you for that, so you will remember the rule and not break it again." The punishment would then be something directed to the actual offense, and tempered by Georgie's telling the truth.

If you can accept the notion that discipline is trying to teach the child *the sense in acting in a certain way*, you must carefully build an understanding of how important it is that people be able to trust you. You explain, not once, but again and again, in varying words, "If you don't tell the truth, someday, when it is really important for people to believe you, they won't."

You read stories that point up this lesson — *The Boy Who*

Cried Wolf, for example. You discuss together TV shows in which this point is made. Only when he really understands the value of one's "good name" will your child see the sense in telling the truth, even when it hurts.

If, in spite of your best efforts, your child repeatedly lies, look for the underlying cause. Often lying is a signal for attention. Eloise lies about her father's job, or the exotic presents she received for her birthday, in a pathetic attempt to win friends. Ruben tells a whopper about where he was when he came home two hours late, which may be saying, "I have to remind you that I am here. You have been too busy lately to notice me."

Stealing

Stealing is a very close relative of lying. When the first attempts to extend the limits of truth are ignored, or accepted with inappropriate punishment, it is an easy next step to stealing. As with all misdemeanors, the age of the culprit is the first consideration. Every nursery school teacher soon learns that there are some children who need to turn out their pockets daily before going home. They will have a collection of small pieces of games and puzzles, little cars and other memorabilia. If it belongs to the school, it is a matter of drawing a line between "what is mine to play with here, and what I brought from home." If it has been taken from another child, it calls for a different conversation, but it would be a mistake to make a big deal of it in the beginning. Repeated offenses would suggest that there might be a cause which should be explored.

The older child who is fully aware of what she is doing when she slips a few candy bars or a small toy into her pocket in the store and walks out without paying, is again testing, not her parents, but the rules of society. When it is discovered, it is wise to take immediate action. The parent need not yell, scream, or threaten to call the cops. A calm, matter of fact but very positive approach will be more effective. When you take her back to the store to admit her misdemeanor and make restitution, that is her punishment. The real challenge to the parent is to try to discover the reason behind the act and to **COMMUNICATE** with the child, helping her to understand what she did was wrong.

Just as your children learn from your bad examples, you can also teach what is right. Most parents have innumerable chances to show their children that you do not take or keep what is not yours.

Elivia and her friend took their children to a movie and for ice cream afterwards. She paid the check as they left, at the same time continuing her conversation with her friend. Before they reached the car she stopped short and said, "Wait a minute. I just realized I only paid four dollars and twenty-five cents. That can't have been right, for four of us. Why, Jesse's banana split alone was two-fifty."

The harried clerk watched anxiously as the entire procession of moms and kids came back into the store. Busy with other customers, he thought that she was returning to complain about an overcharge. When he realized that Elivia was trying to rectify an undercharged bill, he grinned in relief and gratitude. The children listened wide-eyed throughout the entire exchange. A much more positive lesson was achieved than if Elivia had told everyone to wait by the car.

Unacceptable Language

"How would you like to go with me to feed the ducks?" the young teacher asked Terri, a pixie-like three-year-old.

Trustingly, Terri took the teacher's hand and they walked to the edge of the pond, carrying a bag of stale bread.

As they approached, the ducks came swimming rapidly to the shore and waddled out of the pond, quacking loudly.

Terrified, Terri literally climbed up the teacher's legs screaming, "Jesus Christ, the fuckin' ducks will get me!"

Does it shock you to think of a three-year-old child using these words? Of course it does, because at your age, and with your life experience, you have acquired knowledge of their meaning and an attitude toward their use. To Terri, such words were as commonplace as bread and butter, chair or window. They were the common vernacular of her home and the neighborhood. They were the words people used to express fear, anger or distress.

The teacher reacted wisely. Ignoring the explosive language she directed her attention to comforting and soothing Terri, assuring the frightened little girl that the ducks would not harm her. When Terri finally was coaxed to hold out a piece of bread, her terror turned to glee as she watched the ducks gobble down their food and waddle back into the pond.

Later in the day, this young teacher described the incident to her director and asked whether she had handled it properly. "Yes," the director said, "especially since this was Terri's first day. Her language does pose a problem. If she uses words like that very often the other children are likely to copy her, and if they repeat them at home I will probably have complaints from the parents."

"What on earth will you tell them?" she was asked.

"Well, I will probably say, 'We are aware of the situation and are working on it. We believe that in time we can teach Terri that such words are unacceptable, but we think it is important to do this without making her feel guilty because she doesn't know that they are wrong.'

"Now," she went on, "let's think about how we can deal with it here in school. I suggest that we should move cautiously. This is a case where we remind ourselves of one of the basic rules of learning: start where the learner is. Our children, when they come to this center, bring with them more than a blanket and an extra set of clothing. They also bring values and customs which they have learned from their environment. We certainly cannot tell Terri that she is naughty or that those words are bad, because she probably hears adults say them frequently. Instead, we will have to be creative in thinking of ways to change her language patterns. I don't really see this as a discipline problem, because there was no deliberate intent. If Terri were older and was doing this as a means of getting attention it would be a different matter. Helping this child will be a *slow, bit-by-bit, time consuming process.*

"Now, back to Terri. The day will come when we can tell her that some words are not acceptable here. Give her some language that will serve her need such as: 'You are angry! Tell Chen you are mad!' 'You are frightened! Say "I'm scared!"' 'You can tell Craig that you wanted that toy. Ask him to give it to you after he has a turn.'"

We can excuse vulgar language from children who are too young to have learned the meaning of the words they use so glibly. What about the older child who does know the difference? We are seeing this comprehension at earlier stages than ever before.

A fourth grade teacher took a bold approach. We might say she met fire with fire.

"Teacher, Vena called me an asshole," Rosita complained.

"That wasn't very nice of her. I can see it made you feel bad. Why don't you sit down and work on this puzzle with Shelley?" Ms. Jones answered, in a matter of fact tone.

Quietly, Ms. Jicka took Vena aside.

"You called Rosita an asshole," she stated.

Vena's eyes opened wide with horror. She couldn't believe that her teacher had actually said that word.

"Would you call me an asshole?" Ms. Jicka asked.

"No!" Vena shook her head violently.

"Would you call your mother an asshole?"

"No way! She'd kill me!" was the quick response.

"Would you call Mr. Vanni, the principal, an asshole?" was the next question.

The mere thought brought such a shocked expression to Vena's face that Ms. Jicka had difficulty maintaining her serious expression.

"Well, if you wouldn't say it to any of these people, it must not be a very good word and I don't think you want to say it to your friends."

Ms. Jicka dropped the matter there. She did not berate Vena, or require her to apologize to Rosita. This child was in the fourth grade. She knew that her language was "off limits" but she enjoyed the reaction she knew would be forthcoming when she teased Rosita.

Chuck, a sixth grader, had sprinkled the offensive words of the street liberally through his daily conversation. He knew what he was doing. In a sense he was establishing his identity as a tough kid. In his case, there was only one way to respond. A flat statement, "Your language is offensive. There are plenty of good words in the English language to express your feelings. If you don't know any, I will help you find some, but I cannot let you talk that way in school. What you are doing is just as bad as punching and hitting. When you attack the ears of the people around you, you interfere with their rights."

Although the incidents described happened in school, the problem is just as prevalent in the home. Some parents take a "Do as I say, not as I do" attitude, punishing their children for using the words they utter frequently themselves. Others overreact when their children repeat offensive words that they have heard on the outside. A calm, matter of fact statement, "Daddy and I don't like those words. We don't use them and we don't want you to," will be more effective than an angry scene. Children are quick to recognize and capitalize on behavior that will stir up excitement.

Bathroom Talk

There is a stage, usually at about four, when children are addicted to bathroom talk.

"My kids are in that stage," the teacher of the four's piped up. "They get so silly."

"There is an explanation," the director replied. "These children are just discovering the power of language. They have a great need to play with words, roll them off their tongues, and when they discover a few that will incite a response they use them to the hilt! We can give them songs and poems that have a lot of syllables without any particular meaning. It always amazes me that they learn them so quickly. When *Mary Poppins* was popular, even the very young children could rattle off 'Supercalifragilisticexpialidocious' and I still can't remember it!"

One teacher kept a copy of Edward Lear's *Nonsense Alphabet* close by, and when language began to get raunchy she would gather the children around her and read the verses slowly, taking time for a good laugh over each one.

Nonsense Alphabet

a

A was once an apple pie,
Pidy,
Widy,
Tidy,
Pidy,
Nice insidy,
Apple pie!

b

B was once a little bear,
Beary
Wary,
Hairy,
Beary,
Taky cary,
Little bear!

c

C was once a little cake,
Caky,
Baky,
Maky,
Caky,
Taky caky,
Little cake!

Throwing

The preschool teacher was startled by a piercing scream.
A three-year-old came running toward her, blood streaming
from a gash over her eye.

Alarmed, and feeling somewhat guilty because she had
not seen the incident, Faith picked Sara Jane up, crying "What
happened?"

"Dana hit her with a rock!" the other children volunteered.

"Dana, I'll see you later," Faith said in an angry voice as
she hurried into the building for first aid for Sara Jane.

When she returned with Sara Jane, who was proudly displaying a bandaged head, she took Dana by the hand and sat down beside him. "That was a naughty thing you did, Dana," she began. "You hurt Sara Jane! That stone almost hit her in the eye. It could have made her blind! You know what I have said about throwing stones! Why did you do it?"

Dana, whose anxiety had been growing while Sara Jane was gone, burst into tears. "I didn't throw the stone at Sara Jane!" he sobbed. "She is my friend. I wouldn't hurt her! I just picked up the stone and throwed it. When I grow big I want to be a baseball pitcher, and Daddy said to practice throwing!"

"Well, throwing is fun, but we do have to be careful what we throw and where we throw it."

Faith set up several games which gave the children legitimate reasons for throwing. She brought an old bedspread from home and suspended it on a rope between two posts and painted a target on it. The little ones were satisfied with just throwing a ball against it, but the older children practiced for accuracy and kept score. She also created an area where the children could throw wet sand against the side of the building, a very different throwing experience.

She made a game of tossing a ball into a wastebasket, emphasizing the difference between tossing and throwing.

In a safe area on the playground, she set up a tin can as a target and the children tried to knock it off with stones. In all of her games, the rules were explicit. All participants were lined up well behind the person who was throwing. Talking about and making the rules governing safety was an important part of each game.

Frequently, when we are disturbed by an act which would be legitimate under different circumstances, we can substitute another activity which will satisfy the child's need. In that case, we can say, "I cannot let you throw stones, or wave around big sticks. Let's see if we can think of things to do without hurting anyone!" Given the challenge, children can often exceed adults in the imaginative games they will contrive!

Faith was dealing with a child who had been hit by accident. Explaining the need to be careful and then offering acceptable ways to throw things, without risk, was an excellent way to handle that particular situation. However, some children do throw things with the intention of hitting someone and a desire to hurt. In many cases the act is instinctive — not premeditated — but that doesn't make it less dangerous. It is important to deal with this firmly and consistently while the child is young. If he is permitted to resolve his conflicts with violence, he may well continue that pattern through adolescence and into adulthood.

The young child needs to be able to lean on the security of knowing that someone will stop her before she hurts anyone. When an adult says, "I will not let you hurt Anja," it is comforting — not threatening.

She learns that feelings are not bad in themselves — it is what we do with them — and that there are ways to express them which will not get her into trouble.

Temper Tantrums

Probably one of the most frightening behavior problems a parent or teacher encounters is the uncontrolled display of temper. Even a tiny baby can frighten the wits out of his parents by holding his breath until he turns purple, and that is the forerunner of increasing displays of temper. The toddler usually uses his vocal cords to make known his demands.

What can you do with a child who is screaming? Clearly this is one time when the firm, calm, direct approach is ineffective.

To say "Your screaming is annoying me and disturbing others" will not make much of an impression if the child who is bellowing cannot hear you. Diversionary tactics are required.

You can offer a toy which may be snatched and thrown across the room. You can try to hug and soothe, and may be bruised in the process. Rosalie told of a technique which she jokingly called the "water treatment."

"Jose was a volatile four-year-old," she recounted, "who could scream longer and louder than any child I have known. One day I put on my most concerned, solicitous expression and offered him a glass of water. I expected that he might dash it out of my hand but instead, with a surprised look he accepted it and gulped it down. Since he couldn't swallow and scream at the same time, I had a chance to talk. 'Your throat must really hurt,' I said, soothingly. 'Now you just have a nice drink and it will feel better. As soon as you have finished we will go find a carrot for Peter Rabbit.' It worked! That time and the next, and the next! My moment of joy came when I saw Jose open his mouth and start to scream. Suddenly he stopped, went over to the sink, and got his own drink of water!"

Recently, when I was sitting on a plane waiting for take-off, a little fellow, rebelling against the restriction of a seat belt, tuned up. As the crescendo of his screams increased, the other passengers were shooting looks of sympathy or annoyance at his embarrassed mother. The flight attendant approached with a glass of water — and it achieved the desired results!

When parents are faced with this problem they should first be aware that there are different kinds of temper tantrums. There are the deliberately contrived scenes where a child throws himself on the floor and kicks and screams in order to have his own way. Whether he wants a candy bar, a new toy, or the desired seat by the window in the family car, it becomes a power struggle, a battle of wills which takes on new dimensions each time it is played. These tantrums usually end abruptly once the desired goal is achieved. If the parent gives in, the demonstration stops. It is hard to turn your back on him if he puts on his act in public and his actions are drawing an audience, but whenever possible this is the best method.

Much more serious are the temper tantrums which take over a child when he is seized by uncontrollable anger. In such a state he is not responsible for his own actions, and may cause serious injury to himself or others or mindless destruction of property. If such tantrums are not curbed in the early years of his life the child becomes more and more of a menace, and less receptive to help.

In this case the attitude of the adult he sees as a role model may play an important part. We have all known men who seem to be proud of their tempers. "Better keep out of my way when you see fire in my eye!" they will say without realizing that the message they are conveying is "Look how big and important I am! See what power I have! Everyone is afraid of me!" Some wives view this as "Macho" and can be heard saying, almost bragging, "My husband has a terrible temper! When he is mad we all clear out of his way!" It is not surprising that children who witness this behavior never learn to make an effort to control their own displays of temper.

Dealing with a violent temper is never easy. A consistent approach, discussed and agreed upon by both parents, will be most effective. We hear a lot about parents who abuse their children physically or emotionally, but very little from the parents who are ashamed to admit that they are actually afraid of their children. A husky well-developed five-year-old who discovers that he can intimidate his mother is in a very scary position. He finds himself at the controls before he has learned to fly.

It takes enormous effort and self-control for the parent or teacher to provide the troubled child with the reassurance of calm, steady, consistent support. Saying "I will not let you do that" is like offering a rope to a drowning victim. Offering positive reinforcement, in the form of justifiable praise when he succeeds in exerting self-control will enable him to pull

himself up that rope. But yelling back at him, responding with an anger as great as his own, or physically punishing him, is to push him down deeper into the depths of his own uncontrolled feelings.

Adults must be objective, not emotional. They need to start when the child is young enough so they can control him physically, not by spanking, but holding him firmly, while speaking in a calm soothing voice. With children old enough to comprehend, a discussion of the problem can be held later, when the child is calm.

For example: "We had a bad time because you lost your temper when Gary wouldn't let you be first. He made you mad and you tried to hurt him. No one has the right to hurt another person. Such behavior is not acceptable."

"Well, I've tried all this," weary parents will say. "For a whole month I have been a model of restraint, but nothing seems to do any good. My child still flies off the handle at the drop of a hat."

The circumstances leading to the behavior probably had been building up for much longer than a month, and the glue which will mend the cracks — calm, quiet, firm, consistent support — will have to be applied, as the old song says, "not for just a day, not for just a year, but always."

CHAPTER 10

Move Over for the New Baby

The nursery room was quiet and peaceful. The children were all asleep on their cots and Louise, their teacher, was just settling down for a moment's rest when suddenly Mercedes, a precocious young lady of three, sat straight up on her cot.

"When that baby comes out of my mother's stomach I am going to shake her, and shake her, and shake her!" she announced in a determined voice, demonstrating her thoughts with violent movements of her arms.

Louise moved quietly over to sit on the floor beside Mercedes' cot. "Tell me about it," she whispered, "but we will have to talk softly so we won't wake the other children."

"Well, if SHE thinks she's going to give that baby MY crib, and all those dresses that were mine when I was a baby — well, SHE'S NOT!"

Louise knew about the pending blessed event. Everyone knew about it. Mercedes had been walking around for weeks with her stomach thrust out, telling the children she was going to have a baby. Her mother had taken her into her confidence almost as soon as she had received the initial news from the doctor, and that had been a mistake. A small child's sense of time is narrow — everything is in the NOW — and the anticipation was too much to bear. It was plain that her mother had painted what she thought was a rosy picture, but Mercedes had different ideas.

How Would You Feel?

"Imagine," said a psychiatrist to a group of teachers and parents, "that you are a bride of one year. Your husband has adored you, doted on you, admired your every act. You have been Queen, the First Lady, the apple of his eye. Now picture him sitting down with his arms around you saying, 'Darling, I have wonderful news for you. Some day soon I am going away for a few days. My mother will stay with you while I am gone, and when I come back I will have a surprise — a NEW BRIDE! Won't that be wonderful? She can sleep in your bed in my room, and you can have a nice big bed and room all of your own. She can wear all of those pretty dresses you had when you were a bride. You can help me take care of her, and when she has been here a while and gets used to us, you can play with her! Isn't that going to be fun?'"

This is the approach so often taken when parents tell their offspring of the advent of a new member in the family. On the surface it may seem sensible, but if we stop to think about the bride's feelings we can begin to empathize with the child who has been receiving all of his parents' attention and is told to "move over." It is ridiculous to imagine that the news will be accepted with delight. It is naive for parents to rule out the possibility of jealousy, lest they fail to notice when gentle patting turns to surreptitious pinching.

Having been forewarned by this story, Matty and Christa found a better way to help their four-year-old son adjust to the arrival of his baby sister. She was still sleeping in a bassinet when they discussed the need for a new crib in Matthew's presence.

"I guess we'll just have to buy a new crib," Christa said.

"Yes, I suppose we will," Matty replied. "Well, there goes the money we had been saving for a vacation."

Matthew, who had been listening attentively, burst forth with, "Dad, I have a great idea! We can give Ashley my crib and I can sleep on a big bed!"

"That is very generous of you," Matty replied, "But are you sure you are ready to sleep in another room all by yourself?"

"Sure," was the confident reply, "and you know that bathtub Mum used to wash me in when I was a baby is still down in the cellar. Ashley could have that too!" Instead of feeling disgruntled and displaced, Matthew became a solicitous, protective big brother.

Sometimes a child who appears to have weathered the arrival of a new baby without any serious reactions will suffer pangs of sibling rivalry when that baby suddenly becomes "cute"; when she takes that first step, says that first word, and is suddenly the center of attention. Billy was a prime example of this delayed reaction.

Delayed Feelings of Jealousy

"We are having some problems with Billy," Ms. Simmons reported to Mrs. Ash. "He has been doing a lot of biting lately, and he seems to be focusing on one particular child. Could you come a little early today when you pick him up so we can talk it over?"

When Mrs. Ash came, her husband was with her. "We have been having a terrible time with Billy at home," she reported. "He has always been such a good kid, and lately he has been obnoxious. He is sneaky, lies, cries, and whines a lot. We didn't realize you were having trouble too, but we are really concerned. Do you suppose there is something physically wrong with him? Why would a child's personality change so drastically? Should we take him to a psychiatrist?"

"How old is your little one?" Ms. Simmons asked.

"Oh, she's fifteen months, and such a doll!" her mother replied, glowing. "She has just started walking, and she is so cute, toddling around."

"Do you think that could be Billy's problem?" was the next question.

"Why would that happen now?" asked Mr. Ash. "We thought we might have problems when she first came home from the hospital, but Billy seemed to accept her very well."

"It is not uncommon for this delayed reaction to occur when the new baby begins to be really cute, and everyone is admiring each new advance in her growth," Ms. Simmons said. "I have never seen her. What does she look like?"

"Melissa has adorable dimples, and blonde curls, and the brightest blue eyes! She does attract a lot of attention, even from strangers when we go out. She is a real ham — plays up to everyone. She bats her eyes at the men like a little flirt!"

"It may be just a coincidence," Ms. Simmons went on. "We should be careful not to jump to conclusions, but the child Billy has bitten several times has blonde, curly hair and blue eyes. It has reached the point where she starts screaming when she sees him coming."

"Oh, that's awful!" Mrs. Ash exclaimed in shocked tones. "The poor thing! It's a wonder her mother hasn't complained!"

"She has," Ms. Simmons said ruefully. "She is a very sensible, understanding person, but I would hate to have to explain one more bite. For the past two days I have had someone staying within arm's reach of Billy, until I could talk to you and see if we could find out what was going on."

Mr. Ash had been quietly listening to most of this, but now he spoke up. "It seems to me we have been pretty blind. I don't know why we didn't see for ourselves what was happening. Anyway, I can see what we have to do. First of all, we stop making so much of the baby in Billy's presence, and we will warn the relatives to tone down their admiration. Then we'll spend some extra time with Billy, let him know he's still very special to us. Maybe we could leave the baby with a sitter and take Billy off with us for the day. He loves to go into the city — ride the elevators, eat in a restaurant. We haven't done that since Melissa was born. What I want to know now is whether we should speak to Billy about biting?"

"Not yet," Ms. Simmons replied. "He is a very bright boy. He knows what he is doing is wrong, and I think if he learns that I have told you about his biting his guilt will only make matters worse. Let's see what happens when you can put some of your ideas into effect. I will continue to monitor the situation here."

Covering Up Jealousy

Jealousy of a new baby will crop up in different ways and at different times, but it always stems from the same source — the feeling that the child has been pushed aside and is no longer of first importance to his parents. Danny had succeeded in concealing his anxiety from his parents but it did show up in his behavior at school.

"Is anything unusual going on in your home?" Ms. Lawson asked in a phone call to Danny's mother. "Danny has been acting in a very disruptive way for a week now, not at all like his usual self."

"Why no, we haven't seen anything different at home," Mrs. Jacobs replied. "I'm sorry if he is giving you trouble. I will talk to him about it when he comes home."

"Please don't. Let's give it a little time and see if we can find out what's going on. Do you think it might have anything to do with the new baby?"

"I'm sure it isn't that," Mrs. Jacobs replied emphatically. "He adores her. He runs straight to her when he comes in the house and is so gentle and loving with her."

That very afternoon Mrs. Jacobs called Ms. Lawson. Her voice was trembling. "I'm literally shaking," she reported. "I can't believe what just happened. I remember what you said at our last parents' meeting about ways of helping children air their true feelings, so I asked Danny if he would like to write a letter to his grandmother. Of course, I was doing the writing, but let me read to you what he said.

"Dear Nanny,

There is a greenhouse at my school. Behind the green-house is a bush with poison berries. I am going to pick some of the poison berries and give them to Suzanne."

"I'm glad one of the methods I suggested has helped you to understand Danny's feelings," responded Ms. Lawson.

Teachers deal with many children and a wide range of problems. They can be more objective about looking at causes and seeking solutions. They can apply their learning and note the results. If one thing doesn't work, they can try another approach.

Parents are more emotionally involved when a behavioral problem appears. Their experience usually is limited to their own children, and very often they have never read or studied child development, so they do not have the comfort that comes from knowing that certain behavior is to be expected at a certain age. This is one area in which they can benefit from the advice of teachers who have studied child growth and development. Parents and teachers can learn from each other; they can look at behavior from different perspectives.

Ms. Lawson suggested a simple technique to Danny's mother, a tool to help him express the thoughts that were troubling him. She stressed that it was important for her to maintain her position as a "non-person," to convey the impression that she was just a machine recording his thoughts. If Mrs. Jacobs had stopped in shocked disbelief and berated Danny for having such wicked ideas, she would have slammed the lid on his emotions, pushing them down inside where they could fester and erupt in another way.

The question arises as to how the mother could be so deceived about Danny. What about the "gentle, loving" child who "adores" his baby sister?

Parents often delude themselves into seeing what they want to see. Children know what their parents want and expect and what pleases them. How often had this mother said to visiting relatives and friends, "It's just wonderful the way Danny loves Suzanne. He can't wait to see her when he comes in."

If Danny really adored the baby, he wouldn't want to hurt her. Isn't it more likely that he runs straight to the baby checking to see if she is still there? Who knows, she might have vanished as mysteriously as she appeared, leaving Danny supreme again.

What else might have helped ease the pain of this displacement for Danny? Let's go back to one of those key words: **ANTICIPATE**.

Make the Child a Part of the Planning

Long before the baby comes, there are some steps you can take.

First let us consider how you can help a small child understand that when you take care of something it becomes more interesting and more important to you as time goes on?

One way is by planting a seed in a cup and watching it grow. "Those tiny brown seeds aren't very exciting or beautiful," you can point out, "but we will take care of them,

give them water and sunshine and they will become beautiful flowers or delicious green peas. Our baby won't look like much at first, but we will take care of her and she will grow into a big, strong, handsome child, just like you!"

Books can help. Read stories aloud about sisters and brothers who have good times together, with comments like, "Before you can have a brother big enough to do these things with you, we have to have a baby. The baby has eyes and ears and little tiny fingers, but he needs us to take care of him until he can walk and talk and play games with you."

Establish the practice of including the child in some of the things you have to do around the house. Pushing a vacuum cleaner, dusting, washing the car, and raking leaves are all within the capabilities of a three- or four-year-old. Sure, it takes patience. It is much easier and faster to do it yourself, but it gives him a sense of importance, and when the new baby comes this will be time you spend together, times when that "intruder" is excluded.

It is a very good idea before the baby comes to develop a routine that is special to the child. A "read aloud" time, or regular outings with Daddy. Whatever it is, make time for it. It is important to continue this relationship after the baby arrives. This is a way of saying "Yes, there have been some changes in our family, but YOU are still important to me!"

After the big event, try to be matter of fact about the new baby when the child is present. Let him share in the responsibility for the care of the baby as he shows an interest and desire, but do not make it a burden.

Praise the child honestly when he is really helpful — like bringing you a clean diaper, rocking a cradle, holding a bottle, talking or singing to the baby. (In a child care center, the caregivers were amazed to see an infant stop crying when a four-year-old stood by the crib and sang to him. It was a toss-up as to who gained the most; the baby, the child who was being helpful, or the teacher!)

Share with her your memories of her infancy. "When you first came home from the hospital, you were just about this size. You were such a beautiful baby. Daddy and I were so proud of you. I used to sit in that chair right over there and rock you, and sing to you, and look at your perfect little fingernails, and your nice flat little ears." As you say these things, you are letting her feel special while at the same time you draw her attention to the things that make the new baby special.

When you have to make an older child wait because you are changing or feeding the baby, explain that you will attend to his needs as soon as possible. And then be sure that you do.

What has all this to do with discipline? We have already stressed that feelings are at the root of all situations calling for disciplinary action, and jealousy of the new baby is probably the most common cause for unacceptable or inexplicable behavior in very young children. I believe it is a mistake to think that a child will not feel some emotion when he is pushed aside by the newcomer.

Many children deal with it by reverting to baby ways. They may suck their thumbs, talk baby talk, have toilet accidents or ask for a bottle. This is confusing and sometimes embarrassing for the adults, who react with, "How could you wet your pants! You haven't done that for a long time. You are too big to do such a baby thing!"

"Take your finger out of your mouth. Don't be a baby!"

"No, you can't sit on my lap. You are too big!"

"Of course you can't have your milk in a bottle. What if someone should see you! They would laugh at you, a big girl like you!"

It is irritating, but the parent who gives in and goes along with it, constantly seeking ways to make the displaced child feel important and needed, will find that the problem does not last long.

CHAPTER 11

Grown-Ups Goof Too!

Can you keep cool, calm and collected when your children annoy you? Do you stop to weigh your words carefully before admonishing them? Do you maintain a consistently warm, understanding relationship even when they disobey you, talk back, or ignore your directives?

If you can answer "Yes" then fold up your wings and skip to the next chapter. To the other 99% of my readers, I hope to offer comfort and reassurance. You are not failures as teachers or parents. You are average, normal human beings with all the usual combinations of strengths and weaknesses. My aim is to help you recognize and acknowledge the problems you may be creating for yourself, and to plant a few ideas which will help you avoid them.

Working with children is like walking through an open field. On the good days you tread buoyantly over even ground and the grass is soft beneath your feet. And then there comes a day when you stumble into the pitfalls of your own bloopers; when you get caught in a maze of rhetoric and can't find your way out, or when you come smack up against a hard rock of confrontation.

What are some of these common mistakes?

Making Threats You Can't Carry Out

One is making threats you can't carry out.

"Linda Jacobs, if you don't stop fooling around and get your things on, the school bus will go without you!" the exasperated teacher hears herself saying when she knows full well Linda will *have* to be on that bus, even if she has to dress her and carry her on!

"Now you kids better get this mess cleaned up in five minutes or we won't go to the show!" Mother states in un-equivocal tones. But she has already paid for the tickets, and besides, she wants to see the show herself. What will she do?

"How many times do I have to tell you to get in here and get washed?" Mother screams at the twins. "Now hurry up, or we won't go to Grandma's."

If she had been thinking straight she would have known that her lively four-year-olds would far rather stay home and play in their own backyard. Her threat would not get them ready, nor would it put them in a mood to be agreeable when they did get to Grandma's.

Nadia, a three-year-old in a child care center, learned at an early age that threats can boomerang, and at the same time gave her teachers a clear picture of the way her mother han-dled frustration.

"I'll be the mother and you be my kids," she announced to her friends, and immediately, adopting a strident nagging tone, she shouted, "It's bedtime! Get up those stairs to bed!"

Her playmates stood and looked at her, making no move to walk in the direction she was pointing.

"I said go to bed!" she berated them, hands on hips and eyes flashing. "I'll give you until I count ten to get up those stairs. One! Two! Three! Four!" When she reached twelve and no one had moved, she hesitated a moment and then, clapping her hands over her ears, she screamed, "Oh, God, Oh, God! That baby is crying again!"

Ruth, a fourth grade teacher, issued a threat and was caught in a trap of her own making.

'When I *do* it, you *say* it!" she shouted.

As she stood, red-faced and angry, looking into the grinning faces of her class, she heard her own words echoing in her mind. Like a pricked balloon the tension which had been gradually building throughout the morning was dissolved in a burst of hilarious laughter.

If Ruth had said, as she meant to, "When I say it, you do it!" she would have been implying a threat, and an "or else." Sue Spayth Riley makes the point in her book, *How to Generate Values in Young Children,* that when an adult gives an "or else" she is putting the child in the position of making a choice.

An attorney, noted for his ability to select a jury through skillful cross examination, was not quite as clever when it came to second-guessing his seven-year-old daughter.

"What are you doing with that hose?" he shouted angrily as he drove into the yard in time to see Paula direct a stream from the garden hose toward her brother. "How many times do I have to tell you that the hose is not a toy?"

With an impish grin, Paula turned toward her father.

"Don't you dare turn that hose on me!" he bellowed, thus offering a choice. The threat became a suggestion.

Paula thought quickly, Would it be worth it to see her father drenched, and take the punishment that would be sure to follow?

Her decision was to have her fun and take the consequences and as she related her story years later, she chuckled at the memory of her father standing in shocked amazement with water streaming from his pinstriped suit!

Out on a Limb

What can you do when you find yourself out on a limb? It doesn't help to change the subject, as little Nadia did, but it is risky for an adult to challenge the child to call your bluff.

If there is nothing humorous about the situation, retract at once! The longer you wait, the harder it will be.

Ruth did this, and taught her students a valuable lesson at the same time, when she said, "Well, even if I hadn't said that backwards, it would have been a dumb thing to say. You see, I was angry, and even grownups, when they are angry, say things they don't really mean. My mistake was so silly we couldn't do anything but laugh, but it isn't always that easy. Sometimes it takes courage to say 'I was wrong.'"

Offering Choices When There Are No Choices

Closely related to threatening is the error of offering choices when we have already predetermined the answer.

The teacher asks sweetly, "Would you like to hear a story?" and is left in a quandary when she receives a chorus of "no's." Since it was her intent to have everyone sit down in one place and listen, she should have said as she spread a blanket on the floor, "Now we will all sit right here on this story carpet and I will read this new book."

"Do you want to go shopping with me?" Mother asks.

She knows there is no alternative. She has no intention of leaving seven-year-old Andreas alone. Instead she might say:

"We will be going shopping in half an hour. I need you to help me with the bundles," making it very clear that she was not offering a choice.

On the other hand, decision making is an important part of growing up and we need to give our children many opportunities to practice. There are not many legitimate choices for very young children but with a little thought we can create them.

"Do you want the plaid skirt or the green jumper?"

"Will you have pears or sliced peaches?"

"Which crayon will you choose for your picture?"

"Do you want to hear my story or will you sit down over at the table and do some pasting and cutting?"

"Do you want to watch Sesame Street or help me make the dessert?"

At the same time it is the responsibility of the adult to set some very firm limits. "You may do this or this but you cannot do that. This time I will decide. Each year that you are older you will be able to make more choices. Some day you will be making all of the decisions, but you need to have lots of practice first."

One step toward that is for the child to acknowledge that a mistake has been made and that the alternative choice would have been wiser.

Eight-year-old Fahad was given a choice between using his birthday money to go to the circus or buying a toy that had been promoted on TV. He chose the toy, which turned out to be shoddy and broke the first day. Fahad said sadly, "I didn't make a very good choice, Dad, did I?"

"I guess you're right," his father replied. "Your birthday money is gone, but I am proud that you were able to see your mistake and admit it."

"If it is a party, I really think you should wear a dress," Sarah's mother said. "Oh, Mother, you just don't know!" was the indignant reply. "All the kids will wear jeans." Crestfallen, she admitted later that she had made a poor choice. "I really wanted to come home. The others had on their best party clothes."

My own mother helped me learn a lesson when I was thirteen that stuck with me through a whole lifetime of choice making. We were shopping for a new winter coat, and I was enamored of one which was shoddily made and trimmed with fake fur. She warned me that this coat would probably have to do me for two seasons, but I held out for my choice, and she let me make the mistake. The first time I wore it a classmate fingered the collar and said in a snide tone, "Is that cotton?" For most of that year I squeezed into my old coat which was too small, or shivered in a spring coat over two sweaters.

The "Put Down" Destroys the I AM

Art Linkletter wrote a book called *Children Say the Darndest Things!* I wish someone would write another entitled, *Grown-Ups Say the Meanest Things!*

Many adults blunder along with very little consideration of the feelings of the children they criticize.

If we want our children to grow into self-confident people who are capable of making decisions, we need to guard against the careless words or thoughtless acts which leave permanent scars on fragile egos. Many of us have suffered through at least one such incident in our developing years.

Johanna was an excellent kindergarten teacher. "I don't know how she does it," the student teacher exclaimed. "I have never seen anyone who talked so little and yet I learned so much in her classroom. The children like and respect her. They all seem to know just what is expected of them, and go happily about their business without anyone standing around telling them what to do. Her program is terrific. There is so much good learning taking place all of the time!"

"Yes, but have you noticed how she freezes when a visitor comes into the room?" a second teacher asked. "She seems to drop a mask over her face that is nothing like the way she looks when she is alone with the children. Some of the parents complain about her. They think she must be cross with the children, but they never see her the way she really is."

When the director asked Johanna to make a brief presentation of her program at a parent meeting, she was met with an emphatic refusal.

"I can't do it!" she said, with a look of desperation. "Please don't ask me to. I will literally be sick!" Then she broke down and related an incident which had occurred when she was in the sixth grade.

"I was always shy," she said, "so when the teacher told me to stand before the class and give a three minute speech on any subject — right off the top of my head — I was terrified. After I had stumbled and mumbled through it she proceeded to ridicule me. She didn't restrict her comments to my performance. She made fun of my appearance, my posture and my stuttering. I was devastated and, as a result, all my life I have had trouble communicating with adults."

I could understand what had happened to this teacher because I had a similar experience at about the same age. The socially acceptable routine in the small New England town where I grew up was to attend the Thursday afternoon dance class. It was the highlight of the week for me. I wore a party dress to school that afternoon and carried my party shoes in a cloth bag. When school was over, I met my friends, also curled, sashed and beribboned, at the Elks Hall where the class was conducted. There we changed into our party shoes, self-consciously pretending to ignore the boys, who stood with clean faces, hair neatly combed and attired in their Sunday best.

The first thing we did was to march around the hall, pausing in front of Miss Fern, our teacher, for a greeting. The little girls learned how to curtsy, the boys to shake hands. I had a secret crush on Miss Fern. I can see her now. She had curly hair and shiny brown eyes, and she always wore a white silk blouse with a short, pleated black skirt. I adored her until one day, as we were learning the intricacies of a Grand March, she called across the floor in a sharp tone, "Grace! You are out of step again! Don't you know which is your left foot?" Somehow I managed to get through that day, but no amount of persuasion could make me go back, and I couldn't even make myself tell my mother why. I'm sure Miss Fern didn't know that her thoughtless words had left such an impression but to this day I can't quite forgive her for the wound she inflicted. In time it was covered with scar tissue, but the pain remained. All through high school and college I agonized over proms and dances. I could dance up a storm in my own room — but when I reached the dance floor, suddenly I had two left feet!

Comparison and Competition

Another common mistake made by adults is to pit one child against another, forgetting that each one is unique, and progresses at his own rate.

Sometimes parents think the way to motivate their children to greater effort is to sing the praises of one when talking to the other. Stan and Ken were married adults with children of their own before they made the discovery that their well-intentioned father had almost succeeded in making them despise each other. Riding home from a ballgame, they began to speak freely.

"What always gets me," Stan said, "is that when Dad comes to visit us he spends the whole time telling us how successful you are, how big your house is, how smart your kids are. By the time he leaves I feel like nothing."

Ken stared at him incredulously! "But that's exactly what he does to me!" he responded. "I grew up with the idea that I could never measure up to you in his estimation! I remember once when I told him about a promotion, instead of congratulating me, he went right into a story about your new office and the bonus you got!"

When you constantly compare one child with another, you succeed in making him feel inadequate, weaken his I AM and set his developing I CAN into reverse!

"Come out in the yard when you finish supper," Zachary's father said. "I'm going to teach you how to stand up and hit that baseball if it takes me all night! I'm sick of having that brother of mine telling me what a great player your cousin is!" Taking time out to play ball with his son would be commendable, but in this case his motivation soured the whole experience.

"Katy Sullivan called today," Mother said at the dinner table. "She pretended that she wanted a recipe, but she really wanted to tell me her Katherine brought home a report card with five A's. I wouldn't give her the satisfaction of telling her what you got, Moira, I was too ashamed. I know you are just as smart as Katherine. You just aren't trying hard enough. I think we will have to cut out all television until you can do better!"

If television were really interfering with Moira's completion of her homework, taking away some of her viewing time might have been a logical punishment. To expect her to match the performance of another child was unfair.

"But we live in a highly competitive society!" I hear someone saying. "We must train our children to compete or they will get buried when they get out into the real world."

In this book, I am talking about children up to about eight or nine years old. In those years they have so much growing and learning to do that we hamper them when we add the emotional strain of competition with their peers. Instead, encourage each child to compete against his own record.

"Today you swam across the width of the pool. Next you can try to swim the length!"

Bribes and Rewards

When and how are they effective? To offer a bribe before the deed is accomplished puts a great strain on the child. "If you don't cry at the dentist's I will buy you that model airplane," adds one more burden to an already overloaded circuit. Wait until the session is over and then say, "You really were brave! I was proud of you. Let's go buy that model plane!"

Bribes are like blackmail. The demands increase until the parent is buying behavior which should be taken for granted.

On the other hand, a prize is all the sweeter when it has been honestly earned. It doesn't always have to be something to hold in your hand. A word of praise, a pat on the shoulder, or a quick hug indicates approval and builds self-confidence.

Gold Stars

One form of rewarding a child for behavior is to offer a visible reward, such as a gold star placed on a chart or stuck on the back of his hand. This method seems to work, for a while, but it is like applying a bandaid without first cleaning the wound. Self discipline is not something you can paste on a child's exterior; it comes from within when he *sees the sense* in being good and wants to be good.

Rewarding a child with a gold star for brushing her teeth is belittling her intelligence and we all like to believe our children are smart. A few words of praise, "Your teeth look shiny clean, you must have been brushing them every day," or of appreciation, "Thank you for picking up your toys so I could vacuum your rug," will give your child an inner glow which far surpasses the effect of the gold star.

Manners

Of course we all dream of showing the world a courteous, polite, well-mannered child, but let's put first things first. Is our own pride at stake? Do we want "them" to give us brownie credits for training our children in social graces? Or do we want to help our children apply the lubrication which will smooth their way through an aggressive, critical, and often antagonistic world? To pressure children to mouth the words "please," "thank you," and "excuse me" without any comprehension of their meaning is like feeding them butter without the bread. Good manners grow out of feelings and concern for the welfare of others. We can, however, establish a respectful climate in our homes. When a child asks for something, we do not have to get coy and demand the "magic word." A quiet "please" as you hand it to him, followed by "thank you" if he doesn't say it first, will suffice. But when he does say it, without any prompting from you, compliment him. "You remembered to say 'please'! You are really growing up!"

Demanding Apologies

"You apologize to your sister right now," Mrs. Jewett screamed at her eight-year-old son, Roger. "You broke her new skateboard. Tell her you're sorry!"

Roger stood there with a mutinous expression, glaring at his sister Ruby. "She left it in the way," he muttered. "Can I help it if she's stupid?"

Ruby interrupted her wailing with an indignant cry. "You're a clumsy fool!" she screamed. "Why can't you look where you're going?"

"Never mind that," her mother yelled. "I said to apologize and I mean it!"

Still no answer from Roger.

"O.K. then, you're going to sit right in that chair until you apologize."

Five minutes later, realizing that he couldn't win, Roger muttered, "I'm sorry" and ran into his room, slamming the door.

Was he sorry? Of course not. What did he learn? That grown-ups are unfair, but because they are bigger and stronger, they hold the power. A basic lesson in the theory that "might is right."

Moesha, a teacher in a child care center, felt that children should be made to apologize.

When three-year-old Therese snatched Emeka's paper and ripped it in two, Moesha grabbed her by the arm.

"That was a naughty thing you did," she shouted. "You made Emeka cry! He was going to take that paper to his mother. Now you tell him you are sorry. Apologize to Emeka!"

The word was unfamiliar and incomprehensible to Therese, who made no attempt to comply.

Taking her into the foyer where the receptionist was working, Moesha sat Therese down hard, saying in a cross tone, "Now you sit right there until you are ready to apologize," and went back to her group. She came back several times to say, "When you are ready to say you are sorry, you can come back with us." Therese did not respond, either with tears or anger. Instead she used her own defense weapon — she messed her pants!

Later, when she was reproached for her actions, Moesha was defensive. "Kids have to learn to say they are sorry, and it is our job to teach them," she insisted.

There are many parents, and teachers, who would agree with her. They believe that forcing children to "mouth" the words will teach them to be sorry. Actually, what they learn is that when you are small it is better to do what "they" tell you to, or you will be punished. In short, they are being programmed to be hypocritical.

Therese was only three, and it was unlikely that this incident did any lasting damage, but Giorgio, a fifth grader, had already developed his own set of values.

"Giorgio is in the office," the teacher's aide reported to the fifth grade teacher. "He was very rude to me and he refused to apologize."

Before Mrs. Duval could question the young aide further, Giorgio came into the room. He handed her the office pass and went to his desk where he slumped into a chair, his face dark with anger.

Mrs. Duval ignored him while she gave directions to the rest of her class and then pulled a chair over and sat down beside him.

"What happened, Giorgio?" she asked in a low voice.

He looked up angrily. "It wasn't my fault! She started it! She told me to get in line and when I did she yelled at me for getting in the front! So I yelled back! Then she took my baseball cap and said she wouldn't give it back until I apologized! Well, I won't, because it wasn't my fault!" He ended his tirade with, "And she's not keeping my cap!"

Mrs. Duval sighed inwardly. Baseball caps were a symbol. The boys never took them off. She knew that when Ms. White took Giorgio's cap it was the most inflammatory action she could have taken.

"Giorgio," she began, "I understand that you are angry because you think Ms. White was unfair. I wasn't there so I won't talk about what happened, but I do know this. All your life you will run into things which seem unfair and find that you can't do anything about it. The important thing for you to learn is self-control. When you lose your self-control things always get worse."

"I'm not going to apologize," repeated Giorgio, with no sign of weakening. "I hate her!"

"I'm sorry to hear you say that," his teacher replied. "Hate is a very wasteful emotion. It doesn't usually hurt the other person, but it acts like a poison on the one who does the hating."

Giorgio looked up and for the first time there was a gleam of understanding in his eye. "Well, I don't like her!" he said emphatically.

"Ah, now that's all right. You don't have to like everyone. You don't have to like me or Ms. White, or even the principal. However, when people are in authority you do have to accept their orders, even if you disagree with them. I can understand that you really aren't sorry that you talked back to Ms. White, because you meant what you said. However, you lost your self-control. You should always be sorry when that happens. I wonder if you could say that to Ms. White? Not that you admit that she was right but simply that you are sorry you lost your self-control and spoke rudely."

When the school day ended, Giorgio said to Ms. White, "I'm sorry I was rude," and received his cap.

Requiring a child to apologize is a sensitive issue which I have heard debated heatedly at both parents' and teachers' meetings. There will probably be many readers who truly believe that it is right to insist that children utter the correct words, even though they don't mean them. If we are really concerned with helping them, we will seek other avenues, as Mrs. Duval did.

Nagging and Scolding

The last and most common of the deadly sins is that we all *talk too much*!

"How many times do I have to tell you...."

"If I've told you once I've told you a hundred times...."

"I'm not going to tell you once more...."

"...And I mean it!"

Does that sound familiar? Do you wonder that our children learn at an early age to tune us out? Our very words contradict our actions, like the teacher who stands before her class, screaming Q-U-I-E-T!!!

I listened to a teacher in a child care center carrying on a continuous monologue.

"Kurt, put your rubbers on." "Get your rubbers on, Kurt." "Have your got your rubbers on yet, Kurt?"

She went on and on, like water dripping out of a leaky faucet, repeating the same words. If she had listened to a tape recording of her performance she probably would have been amazed. Why hadn't she just walked over to Kurt, handed him his rubbers and encouraged or helped him to put them on? She used up so much of her precious energy with useless "yakking" that it was not surprising that she was exhausted at the end of the day.

There is only a slight difference between this meaningless patter and nagging.

"Have you done your homework?"

"Be sure to hang up your coat."

"Put those toys away. Remember your father fell over them last week!"

"Wash your hands."

"You tracked mud on my clean floor!"

"Stop teasing your sister."

This slides naturally into self-pity.

"I worked so hard to get that nice jacket for you and now you tell me you left it on the playground!"

"I spent all afternoon fixing you a nice dinner and now you don't even finish it!"

But of all the useless verbal exercises in parent-child communications, probably the saddest is the parent who is afraid to say "no"; who engages in lengthy arguments with her children, listening with far too much patience while they rationalize, explain, complain, delay, stall and manipulate her until they win the advantage. Children *do not want* to run the show. They have a right to expect that adults will set some limits and maintain control. It gives them a comfortable feeling of security to know that "they won't let me." When parents abdicate their responsibility, it borders on cruel neglect.

CHAPTER **12**

Call in the Reserves

Don't Hesitate to Ask for Help

Sometimes a disciplinary situation can get so out of hand that the parties involved need the advice of an outside observer -one who can stand to one side and view the problem in an unemotional way. Leah, recently appointed director of the child care center where she had been a teacher, found herself floundering, and was wise enough to call on her supervisor for help. On the day that Denise arrived she saw two lively little boys clambering over the furniture in the front office where a tight-lipped secretary was trying to work.

"Why are those children in here on this beautiful afternoon?" she asked.

"She sent them in!" was the muttered answer. "They spend more time in here with me than they do in the classroom. I don't know how they can expect me to get my work done if I have to play babysitter for those little devils. What am I supposed to say if a parent walks in and asks me what they are doing?"

"I'll take care of them," Denise said quietly, and taking each of the boys by the hand she calmly walked away. "It's such a nice day I think you need to be outside," she said, as she took them back to their teacher who was on the playground.

Later when they were in the office, Leah brought up the incident. "I know you were upset because those boys were inside," she began, "but they have pushed us all beyond the limits of our patience."

"Let's talk about them," Denise replied. "How many hours do they spend here?"

"Better than fifty hours a week. They are the first to arrive in the morning — and usually the last to leave. Their parents work in town, and car pool, so they come together."

"They seem to be bright," Denise said. "Some of their antics and language were highly imaginative."

"Oh, they are bright all right," Leah exclaimed. "What one doesn't think of, the other will. They egg each other on and get into all kinds of mischief."

"How do they get along with the other children?"

"That's part of the problem; they are very popular. The other children admire them and copy their behavior."

"What have you done about it?" Denise asked.

"Well, I've asked their parents to talk to them, but that hasn't seemed to do any good. I think I'll have to tell them tonight that if these boys can't behave, I can't keep them. They are wearing out the staff."

Parents and Teachers Need to Understand Each Other

"I'm afraid that asking these parents to 'speak to' their children is ineffective," said Denise. "Have you thought about how these parents feel? Just imagine what they must be saying to each other as they fight the traffic after working all day."

"I wonder if she's going to greet me again with a list of all the bad things Rick has done today."

"Yeah, I can tell the minute I see her face if they have been bad."

"My kid is no angel but he's not really bad. I'm paying good money. If these teachers were doing their job, there wouldn't be a problem."

"What if she won't keep them? The boss will never give me time off again to look for another center. Besides, I'd hate to admit that my four-year-old has been expelled."

Leah looked chagrined. "I guess I have been thinking only of our side of the problem," she admitted.

"There's something else," Denise went on. "What do you think happens to the boys when they leave here after you have burned their parents' ears with your complaints? Can't you hear them scolding and threatening all the way home? Good child care should support and strengthen parent-child relationships, not destroy them.

Report Something Positive

"Now let's think of some actions you can take. First, instead of greeting their parents with stories of their misdemeanors I want you to have at least one positive thing to tell them every single night for the next week. No matter how devilish the children may have been during the day, keep it to yourself!"

"What if there isn't anything good to say?" protested Leah.

"That will be your challenge. If you really observe them, you will find something. Maybe it will be helping another child. Or putting away something without being told. Or being the first to come when their group is called. Or making a great building in the block center. It doesn't have to be a dramatic incident. If it is positive, the parents will probably enlarge it in their minds anyway. At this point, I expect they are grasping at straws.

"I want you to share this directive with the rest of the staff. They, too, are to look for something good instead of reinforcing the negative by complaining to each other. If you all concentrate on looking for good things to report, I am sure that you will see definite improvement in the children. Just lifting the burden of guilt from the parents' shoulders by not complaining to them every night is bound to help, too. I will call you in a week, and if you are still having trouble, then we may want to ask the parents to come in for a conference.

"Another thing — look at that book on your shelf that tells what four-year-olds are like. Give it to your staff to review, and then plan a staff meeting around *Ages and Stages*. At the same time, take a good look at your program to see how well it is meeting the needs of these bright, active boys. Can it be they are bored?

"Finally, ask your lead teacher to keep a journal on both children. Record every incident, noting the time of day, people involved, what was done about it, and their reactions. We may see some kind of pattern emerge which will help us to work out a solution. If we are going to be responsible for such a large part of their waking hours, we must try very hard to improve on the quality of that time. I particularly want to see what activity they gravitate toward most often. We need to capitalize on their special interests. Perhaps you can give them more of it, or at least try not to take them away when they are truly involved.

"When you have established a better rapport with the parents, you may be able to help them with suggestions for things which they can do at home, based on your knowledge of four-year-olds."

Keeping her word, Denise called Leah one week later.

"How are you getting along with your problem children?" she asked.

"What problem children?" was the cheery response. "We can't believe that there could be so much change in just one week! Your suggestions were so simple — but they worked!"

This is an example of the need for parents and teachers to establish a sympathetic, understanding relationship. Leah was piling unnecessary pressures on the shoulders of harried, working parents who were already feeling guilty. They, in turn, were scolding and punishing their children when they should have been enjoying them in the limited time they shared.

Don't Try to "Wing It" Alone

Single parents who are working and trying to be good parents at the same time feel very lonely. They are usually exhausted because their physical and emotional energy is stretched thin. A truly committed child care director is always ready to lend a listening ear or a comforting shoulder, because she knows it is the child who will ultimately benefit.

Teachers sometimes fail to call upon resources their colleagues and superiors can offer. It is a mistake to try to "wing it" alone when there are people who would be happy to give you the benefit of their experience. Your principal or supervisor will not think less of you for admitting that you have a lot to learn, and everyone likes to be asked for advice!

The responsibility for a growing child is too great to be borne by a single individual. There are reserve sources available to everyone, but most of us are reluctant to seek their advice because we see it as an admission of our own inadequacies. If we are lucky, there are grandmothers waiting to be asked, hesitating for fear they will be accused of interfering. Relatives, friends, neighbors— somewhere among them there is a kindly soul who would be glad to serve as your sounding board.

Who are *your* reserves? Look around you; they are there!

CHAPTER 13

Some Thoughts on Punishment

With our eyes still focused on *helping children to see the sense in acting in a certain way,* we will now explore the place of punishment in discipline.

When the behavior of an individual infringes on the rights of another person, it is a misdemeanor. This boils down to "You may not hurt people," and "You may not destroy property." I would add for good measure "You may not be rude or fresh to adults."

Punishment implies consequences. In simplified terms I talk about "or elses." A child needs to know that something unpleasant will happen if he breaks a rule. With young children this usually means spanking, verbal abuse, isolation or withdrawal of privileges.

Spanking

"I have just as much right to hit you as you have to hit me!" Douglas shouted as he kicked his father in the most sensitive area of his leg — the shin bone. Frank Farrar drew back in surprise and anger. His first reaction was to reach for his five-year-old-son and let him know who was boss, but the ridiculousness of the situation struck him. Here he was, a six foot, one hundred and ninety pound man standing off against a five-year-old-boy who tipped the scales at forty-five pounds. Frank gave himself a second to cool down and then said calmly, "You have a point there, Doug. It was wrong of you to kick me; it hurt like the devil, but it was just as wrong for me to whack you. I expect that hurt, too. Let's talk about it and see if we can't figure out a better way to solve a problem.

"You were wrong to use my tools without permission and now you have spoiled an expensive saw. What do you think would be a fair punishment for what you did?"

(Note: For those who think a five-year old is not capable of deciding on a punishment, let me assure you that years of experience working with young children have shown me that almost always a child will be harsher on himself than an adult would have been.)

In telling me about this, Frank said, "I have to admit I was kind of proud of Doug for having the guts to stand up to me, and it made me think about why I spanked him. I realized that when I do resort to spanking it is usually to relieve my feelings. If I use the old cliche, 'I'm doing this for your own good,' or 'This hurts me more than it hurts you,' it isn't true and he's smart enough to know it!

"If I did something wrong when I was a kid I knew what to expect. My father put me over his knee and gave me a good spanking! When I spank Douglas I'm just carrying on the pattern! I decided then that I had to find other ways to handle discipline. I figured that if Douglas was smart enough to know that spanking didn't make any sense, I could try talking to him as an intelligent human being."

Spanking is a very controversial subject which crops up almost every time I speak to a group of parents on the subject of Discipline. There are always arguments on both sides.

The proponents will say:

"The flat of the hand applied on a child's bottom says, more clearly than words, 'O.K., you have broken the rules and this is the consequence.'" Or,"When I spank my kid it relieves my feelings and lets him know I'm really mad." Or, "A good spanking clears the air!"

After listening to arguments on both sides I reluctantly admit that I spanked my first child — with a hairbrush! — and then go on to say,

"If I could have a second chance, knowing what I do today, I would never lay a hand on any child in punishment!"

Why? To begin with, I would see it as an admission of failure. Child rearing is a constant challenge. I know now that each behavioral problem has a solution. Spanking is a copout for lazy folks who find it easier to REact than to find a better way to ACT. If I had been exposed to the four steps: **ANTICIPATE! HESITATE! INVESTIGATE!** and **COMMUNICATE!** I think I could have been more imaginative in choosing my methods. Parents are TEACHERS and the lesson we teach when we spank a child is that the world is controlled by the strong.

There is a distinction between spanking and a beating. If you really feel that you must use spanking as a punishment, I strongly urge you to choose your weapon with care and consideration. The flat of the hand on a child's bottom will hurt his feelings more than his body. Using a switch, ruler, hairbrush, stick or belt is dangerous, and in a growing number of states, may be illegal. In many cases, the person who needs to punish a child by striking him is carried away by his own emotions. It is too easy to cross over the line from punishment to abuse.

Sixteen year old Gertrude, who had been brought into court for beating her eighteen month baby, said defiantly to the judge, "He was throwing his food on the floor, and I told him not to do it but he looked me right in the eye and did it again, so I hit him — and then I hit him again — and then I couldn't stop hitting him."

Verbal Abuse

There are some parents who say self-righteously that they never hit their child, yet those same parents may use their voices and words in ways that leave more lasting scars than a spanking would. The term "tongue-lashing" sounds threatening, and it is. A loud, angry voice, words that humiliate or degrade, can bring tears to a victim's eyes. A voice which is cold, sarcastic or contemptuous can create a feeling of helplessness.

Sometimes the punishment is more subtle. When Bobby brings home a bad report card and his parent reacts with reproach, Bobby feels guilty as well as ashamed.

Even worse is rejection coupled with threats the parent would never really carry out. "I've had it with your behavior. I'm out of here!" How safe can that child feel? Can she believe she is loved? These approaches are punishment. They do not teach.

Fair and Equal

"You don't love me as much as you do Jeannie," complained six-year-old Jerry to his mother.

"Why, Jerry, how can you say such a thing?" she replied in astonishment. "Of course I love you both the same."

"But you yell at her, and you never yell at me," was his wistful answer.

Jerry was hit by a truck when the twins were four years old. For a time his life hung in the balance, and when he did recover he was left with some minimal brain damage and a permanently crippled leg. Because she had come so close to losing him, his mother had never been able to bring herself to punish him, and he evidently interpreted this as a lack of affection. His perceptive comment made her rethink her attitudes. She had been quick to insist that he be treated like everyone else, but she hadn't been following her own rules. His unexpected reaction was an example of the insight and wisdom children will demonstrate if we take time to listen to their thoughts.

When we set reasonable limits for our children and punish them for their transgressions we convey a message of love. Jerry needed that wonderful secure feeling of knowing that his mother cared for him too much to let his behavior get out of bounds.

How many other times do we treat siblings differently when we punish? Do you know fathers who feel boys need spanking, but would never raise a hand against their daughters?

What about birth order? Sometimes parents treat the first child more strictly, having vowed that they would never let their children get out of control, then ease off as other children come along. Sometimes the reverse is true. By the time the third or fourth child arrives, they decide they have been too lenient and need to be tougher.

Another case of unfair treatment is shown in the following anecdote.

Wearing Two Hats

When Judy saw Mrs. Baker, the center director, approaching with a visiting mother and her child, she glanced apprehensively at her own daughter, Amanda, who was playing happily in the dramatic play corner with two friends.

"Mrs. Easton and Sarah would like to stay awhile," Mrs. Baker said. "Perhaps Sarah can play with the toys while you tell her mother about your program."

Just then Amanda looked up and saw the visitors. Her face clouded over, and within a few seconds there was an outburst from that part of the room. Amanda was holding tightly to Louisa's doll, while Louisa, crying loudly, tried to retrieve it. Amanda was grinning, obviously enjoying her playmate's unhappiness.

"Amanda! Give that doll right back!" Judy admonished in a harsh tone. "You know better than to tease poor Louisa! She had it first."

Now it was Amanda's turn to burst into tears. She flung herself at her mother but Judy pushed her away continuing in an angry voice, "Stop acting like a baby and go play. You can see that I am busy."

"You always blame me! It wasn't my fault! She called me a bad name," Amanda whined. Turning away she went over to a table where four children were working and tried to pull up a chair and sit down.

"You can't sit here!" they said. "You know only four people can sit at this table at the same time."

Amanda ran back to her mother, crying again. "They won't let me play with them," she complained.

"Well, you knew better than to try to sit there," Judy answered crossly. "Now go find something to do. I need to talk to this lady. This is her little girl, Sarah. Sarah might want to come here to school. Why don't you help her find some toys?"

Amanda's answer was to try to crawl into her mother's lap. Judy pushed her away. "Not now, Amanda," she said, more gently. "When we go home you can sit in my lap."

Amanda dragged over a chair and sat as close to Judy as she could. Judy tried to ignore her. Failing to get her attention, Amanda put her hands into her mother's smock pockets. When this didn't work, she began to make small annoying noises.

"It's very hard to have your own child in your class," Judy commented with an apologetic smile.

"I can see that," Mrs. Easton replied. "I think it must be very hard on a child to have to share her mother with so many other children."

When Judy had a break later that day she headed for the director's office. "I have come to give my notice," she announced, her lips quivering. "I love my job but Amanda is driving me up a wall. How is it that I can be so patient and understanding with all of the other children and unable to cope with my own? Mrs. Easton will never want to send Sarah here after what happened this morning. It was awful."

"Yes, she told me about it," Mrs. Baker replied. "I think she could see what was going on, and apparently she was sympathetic to your problem because she did enroll Sarah. Let's talk about it. I don't want to lose you."

"And I don't want to go," Judy said emphatically, "but Amanda has to come first, and she is having a hard time. It is affecting her at home, too. She whines a lot, and a couple of times lately she wet her bed. She stopped that over a year ago."

"I regret that we didn't talk about this when I hired you," Mrs. Baker went on. "I have seen it happen before, and if we had tried to **ANTICIPATE** it we might have saved you both some heartaches.

"The bond between a mother and her child is almost like a permanent umbilical cord. You must try to understand how Amanda feels when she suddenly has to share her mother with a whole roomful of children. She hasn't had the time to develop much emotional strength, and when you push her away, how can she be sure that you aren't forsaking her? It hurts."

"I know you are right," Judy answered, "and I hate myself

for it. I can't go on doing that to my child. The sad part is that Amanda really loves school and she needs the companionship. There is no one in our neighborhood for her to play with.

"My problem is that I am so afraid I will favor her that I lean too far the other way. I don't want the other children or their parents, or even the other teachers to think that I am giving her special privileges, so I never let her be the one to go first, or give the answers, or talk when we have a meeting. I expect her to share, even when she brings something from home. I am really mean to her! Perhaps I can leave and get a job somewhere else so I can afford to keep on sending her here."

"There are a few things we can try before you do anything drastic about leaving," repled Mrs. Baker. "When the children are napping, come back and I will make some suggestions."

Later, when they were able to talk without interruption, Mrs. Baker said, "I should have warned you to talk with Amanda about your new job before you came to work. You could have said something like 'When we go to school, I will be a teacher and I will have to take care of lots of chidren, but I will still be your Mummy, and you will be the *only* one who is *my little girl.*' It would be a mistake to expect her to fully understand what this will mean, but the idea will have been planted, and you can talk more about it when she is faced with sharing your attention. Without the benefit of that advance preparation, let's think of what you can do to handle it now. When she does make demands, I urge you to put up with it. I know it is irritating when she clings to you, cries and whines a lot and wants to sit on your lap. I can understand your frustration when she interrupts and makes a scene because you are paying attention to another child, but it will come out better in the long run if you grin and bear it. Do not scold her or push her away. Try to remember that she is really hurting, and that your rejection is like rubbing salt in the wound. I promise you that it will not last forever. As soon as she is convinced that she comes first in your affection she will not need to test you, and she will be able to get on with the business of play without keeping one eye on you.

"You say that you are afraid that *they* will think you are favoring your own child. Who are *they*? The other teachers? I will talk about this at a staff meeting, and I am sure you will find them sympathetic. Are you worried about the other parents? As long as *you* know that you are being completely fair and that you are not giving Amanda special privileges, you need not be concerned. They are more likely to judge your teaching skills by the way you interact with your own child."

As more and more mothers are looking for part-time jobs to supplement the family income, work in a child care center has many attractive features. Having your own child accompany you eliminates the problem and expense of making outside arrangements, and the hours can often be matched to the school attendance of other children in the family. This seems like a sensible plan, but can present problems, as Judy discovered. However, with Mrs. Baker's advice, she learned that it could be done.

When my first child was four years old, I took him with me to nursery school and I made this mistake. I was so afraid that the other mothers would resent him that I was downright mean. The more I pushed him away, the more he demanded attention with unruly behavior. We were both miserable by the time we walked home at noon. Every day, he ran ahead of me so he could get the hairbrush and hide it! We laugh when this story is told now at family gatherings, but I still harbor feelings of shame and regret.

Isolation and Separation

If we agree that spanking, hitting or screaming are really ways to release the feeling of the adult, what can we do which will bring the desired results? One of the most frequently used methods is isolation. Since the child who is acting up is usually demanding attention, it seems logical to remove him from the scene. It is the way that separation is handled that is important. In the home a parent can send the child to his room; the teacher does not have that option, and some of the alternatives I have observed make me uncomfortable. (I would strongly urge a parent who is investigating child care to ask the director how she handles discipline.)

The "Thinking Chair"

A very common practice is the "thinking chair" or some adaptation of it. In my opinion this is a close cousin to the dunce's stool used by our forefathers. I have often seen children who have been relegated to chairs set apart from the group. Some of them were showing off, gaining the attention they wanted. Some were bored and resigned. I ached for the little ones who were all scrunched up, sad and miserable, and I saw a few who looked like firecrackers ready to explode. The intent of the "thinking chair" is to give the child a chance to think about his misdeed, repent, and decide to do better. It doesn't work that way. When the thinking chair is used to embarrass or humiliate, it loses its purpose. When we say to Suzy, "Sit there until you can behave," we seem to be overlooking the fact that if she could control herself she wouldn't need the chair. The angry child has a tremendous need to let out whatever is causing her trouble, either through words or actions. Leaving her to handle her feelings alone can only intensify the anger, fear or hurt which caused the behavior in the first place.

On the other hand, a "time out place" gives an angry child a chance to cool off. It should be emphasized that time is different in the world of the very young. "Time out" should never be used with children under the age of three, and should last no more than two to three minutes. It might be smart to use a timer so you don't get busy with something else and forget to tell the child to rejoin the group.

Isolation is effective when the focus is on the child rather than his misdeeds. A teacher can say, "You must not be feeling very well today," or "I need you to come over here and calm down; then we can talk. This can be your own special place for a while. No one else can use it until you are through with it."

The special place could be a beanbag chair, a place to crawl into like a blanket over a table, or a large cardboard box lined with soft pillows.

For some children separation is a real punishment. When my own children tested my endurance with their squabbling, I would forbid them to speak to each other for one hour by the clock. Sometimes they went their separate ways, seeking other entertainment, but more often they were pleading for a reprieve before the hour was up.

I watched a teacher in a child care center who dealt with a three year old in this way. He was amusing everyone at the lunch table by spooning his food onto the floor. She quietly took him by the hand, and sat him at another table by himself. She did not berate him for his behavior, scold, or threaten him. The next day she asked, "Do you wish to eat with us today?" and when he nodded assent she made a place for him beside her and the incident was closed. Would that more teachers could talk less and act more!

Withdrawal of Privileges

Another commonly used method for punishing children is the withdrawal of privileges. Here, the main point is to make the punishment fit the crime. It makes sense to take away T.V. viewing time when it is apparent that it has interfered with homework. To use it as a punishment for breaking a dish or another child's toy is not appropriate. The guilty child should have to make reparations in kind. To replace an object, he could give up something of his own of like value.

Consider age. Is the child old enough to understand what he has done and why he is being punished? Children can accept fair and reasonable punishment. They know when they deserve it and they feel better when they pay their dues. They are just as quick to resent unfair treatment. The teacher who keeps the whole class after school, because the kid who hit her with an eraser while her back was turned won't stand up and admit it, is chalking up trouble for herself. If her children lose respect for her they will team up in their efforts to bedevil her.

Helping a child to understand and get rid of the feelings that caused him to misbehave will have more long reaching benefits than punishment. Limits must be set on the methods used, the appropriate place and time to work out feelings and the rules which determine the need. The point to stress is that we can "be the boss of" our own emotions, as Mrs. Carruthers put it so aptly to Joseph. Feelings must not be allowed to become the tail that wags the dog!

Punishment is an ugly word. It has traditionally stood as a symbol of power. A wise parent or teacher will look for alternative ways to deal with people problems. Some of these are described in the following chapter.

CHAPTER 14

An Ounce of Prevention

If you have decided against spanking, if isolation isn't working very well, and if you are worn out with arguments about the withdrawal of privileges, what else can you do? For some answers we turn once more to our definition. It does not say to do something to the child but to help him understand, to make some *sense* out of the reasons for the way people behave.

The first step in bringing about that understanding is to talk openly and honestly about feelings, or emotions. It is important for the child to recognize that we all have strong feelings, both children and grown-ups: everyone feels mad, and sad, and glad and it is all right to do so. Feelings are the propelling force in the developing personality. They provide the contrast that makes life rich and meaningful. Without some grief or sadness one could never truly appreciate happiness. Peace of mind is sweeter when it follows a period of frustration. The person who has suffered loneliness and rejection can recognize and appreciate love all the more when he finds it. Our feelings can work for us or against us. If we deny negative feelings, push them down into the deep dark recesses of the subconscious, they fester and grow like a nasty virus, and sooner or later they erupt and someone gets hurt.

Good feelings need to be exposed also, talked about and demonstrated. There was a song which was popular back in the forties, "Accentuate the Positive!" It was based on what present day educators call positive reinforcement. It is as simple as waking up on a sunny day, feeling great and saying so. It means touching, expressing affection, giving a word of praise, making a positive comment about another's appearance or behavior, thus giving her I AM a spin in the right direction.

We know that our children learn from watching the way we act, and copying the behavior of the adults they most admire. We have a choice. We can teach them to be positive or negative in their outlook.

If you start the day with a doleful, "Another lousy rainy day!" your very words have the power to make the clouds seem darker. If, with a shrug of the shoulder and a knowing expression you intimate that you know something bad about another person, you are not only reinforcing your own derogatory thoughts but it is almost certain that someone will get the message and pass it on, and that the negative aspects will get worse with each retelling.

The power of emotion can be compared with that of the sun. A concentration of its rays on the human body can cause a painful sunburn, or even skin cancer. On the other hand, the sun is a source of warmth and light. When your children are allowed to bask in the light of your approval, they will thrive and grow into healthy self-confident individuals.

Bring the Feelings Out in the Open

Philipe was a very bright creative child whose mental excursions often carried him outside the boundaries of rules. He was not deliberately disobedient or inattentive, but when the wheels were turning inside his active mind he moved in a world of his own, and appeared to be a law unto himself.

In the second grade he encountered a teacher of the "old school" who was determined to squeeze this square peg into the round mold of conformity. It was a classic case of an immovable object coming up against an irresistible force. What Philipe lacked in size he made up for with stubborn determination. Day after day he came home from school in a state of anger and frustration which he usually took out on his younger brother.

His mother, Dorene, wanted him to know that she understood his conflict, but at the same time she knew that he was the one who would have to compromise. It was obvious that his teacher was not going to give an inch.

"It's too bad that you and Mrs. Smith don't get along," she said, "but for as long as you live, there will be people who will not be willing to accept your ideas and the way you think and act. When you get a job you will have to adjust your ways to those of your boss or get fired. And if, someday, you are the boss and have people working for you, there will be times when you will have to practice patience and tolerance; so you might as well start right now. You need to find some legitimate ways to let those angry feelings churning inside you escape before there is an explosion. The trick is to do it at the right time, and in the right place, so you don't hurt anyone or get yourself into more trouble."

The Pressure Cooker

Soon after that something happened which gave Dorene the perfect opportunity to demonstrate to her son what happens when feelings are kept too tightly under control. The lid of her pressure cooker blew off, hitting the ceiling, and spattering its contents all over the wall and floor.

"This is much like what happens to you on the day when Mrs. Smith has leaned on you especially hard," she said. "By the time you get home you are so filled with bad feelings that they explode, just like the pressure cooker, and anyone who gets in your way gets spattered with the hot anger that has been building up inside you.

Dictating Stories and Poems

"When you were little, before you could write, you used to let off steam by dictating stories and poems. I came across one of them the other day that you wrote when you were five. Listen to this:

I'm mad! I'm mad! I'm mad! I am not sad!
Don't come near. Stay away!
You'd better not touch me today!
You hurt me when you squeezed my arm.
Don't tell me to be calm.
You're mean! You're gruff! You think you're tough!
Don't come near.
Stay away!'

"You must have been really mad when you wrote that one. I'm sure you felt better afterward.

"When I was a kindergarten teacher, before you were born, I had a boy named Randy in my class who was giving me a lot of trouble. One day when he had me at my wit's end I sat him down at a table across from me and talked to him."

"You are having a bad day. You hit John and now he won't play with you. You made Diane cry because you snatched the toy she brought from home and hid it. Jim and Steve chased you out of the sandbox because you smashed the castle they were building. Something must have happened to make you feel so mean. Perhaps it would help if you could talk about it, or better still, let's pretend that I am your secretary. You tell me how you feel and I will write it all down."

He just looked at me and shook his head, but I waited.

"Why did you hit John?" I asked, thinking to get him started. That opened the flood gates. For the next five minutes I had to write very fast to keep up with him while his anger poured out.

"They all make fun of me because I wear glasses! They call me four eyes! They wouldn't let me help with their dumb castle! I can make a better castle than they can! You always hang up Diane's papers and you never hang mine! I only wanted to look at her dumb toy, but she wouldn't let me!"

On and on he sputtered. When he finally stopped I said, "Is that all?"

He looked surprised. I guess he thought I was going to scold him. "Shall I read it back to you?" I asked, "That's what a secretary would do." He nodded yes.

I wish I had a videotape of the expressions that crossed his face as I read his words out loud. Alternately he scowled and grinned; he frowned and beamed with approval. Little by little he relaxed.

"What shall I do with it now?" I asked him when I had finished.

"You'd better keep it. I might need it again," was his succinct reply and he went off to play.

Puppets

"Another time I used puppets. I would put one on my hand and give them the other. I gave my puppet a silly name. It was funny but the puppets could say things to each other that the real people couldn't.

"You like to make puppets. Perhaps you can think of a way to use them to express your feelings."

Philipe looked at Dorene thoughtfully but made no comment. It was obvious that she had planted some ideas in his mind.

A few days later Dorene heard Philipe come stamping in, slam the door and go straight to the kitchen. This was one room where the boys were free to use paint or clay and make a mess. He was very quiet for a while. When she heard some sticky plops, she went to **INVESTIGATE**. Philipe had drawn a circle on the wall with a dot in the middle. Before him was a pile of small balls of playdough, which he was throwing at the target. Each time he hit a bulls eye the grin on his face suggested that the dot was Mrs. Smith!

Many people express their anger with an instinctive reaction to throw the nearest object at hand. This isn't limited to children, as the records in any hospital emergency ward would show.

A Punching Bag

A punching bag or a tackling dummy often serves a dual purpose. It may provide exercise when the weather confines active kids indoors, but it also can be a source of release, as Mark's grandmother discovered.

The director of the preschool where Mrs. Stokely had placed her two grandchildren stopped her one day.

"Could you stop for a few minutes after you leave the children?" Ms. Wasilewski asked. Mrs. Stokely returned and when they were comfortably seated, Ms. Wasilewski went on to explain. "I was wondering whether there might be something unusual going on in your home. We have noticed quite a change in Mark's behavior recently."

"What is he doing?" his grandmother asked, anxiously.

"Well, he has always been an energetic little fellow, a typical four-year-old, but lately he has been very rough, hurting other children, and when he is corrected he shouts at the teachers or bursts into tears. I thought you might be able to help us understand what is troubling him."

Mrs. Stokely looked for a moment as if she might burst into tears. "Yes, we are having some problems," she began, "and I don't know how to handle them. As you know, when Jean, my daughter, was divorced she came home to live with us, bringing Mark and little Jeannie. It has not worked out very well. My husband is a retired army officer who believes in strict discipline. He expects so much of the children," she said with a sigh. "They resent it and so does Jean. I feel as if I am in the middle all the time."

"Was he as strict when your own children were small?" Ms. Wasilewski asked.

"Yes, but he was not home much of the time. After the children were in school I thought it best for them to be settled in one place so we did not go with him and when he was on leave they managed to stay out of his way. It's different now. He is home all of the time. He acts more like a drill sergeant than a loving grandfather! He wants them to be quiet and obedient and jump the minute he speaks to them. In a way I can see that it is hard on him. He looked forward to retirement and they do get on his nerves when they act silly or squabble. The other day Mark spilled some paint in Jim's workshop and I thought Jim would have a heart attack. It could be that Mark is missing his father, but he never asks about him so we don't talk about it."

"Perhaps you need to give him a chance to talk," Ms. Wasilewski suggested. "Sometimes we jump to conclusions about what is going on in a child's mind and find that we are way off base."

"There is one thing that has changed," Mrs. Stokely continued. "Jean has started dating again. I don't believe that can be the problem because Mark adores Bill. He would monopolize all of his time when he visits if he could. And Bill is very good about giving him attention. They play ball and sometimes he gets down on the floor and wrestles with him. That irks my husband, too."

"There are a few things I can suggest which might ease the situation, and give Mark an outlet for whatever is really bothering him," Miss Wasilewski offered.

"I'll try anything as long as I can keep him out of Jim's way," Mrs. Stokely replied.

"Why don't you try a punching bag? Stuff a pillow case or laundry bag with old rags and hang it up where the children play. The next time Mark seems upset, you might suggest that he can work out on the punching bag."

Two days later Mrs. Stokely came into the office. "It worked!" she exclaimed. "And you were right. I was jumping

to the wrong conclusion. It wasn't Jim's strictness that was upsetting Mark. The punching bag you suggested gave me the answer," said Mrs. Stokely. "I hung it downstairs in the playroom, and when Mark went down to use it, I sat on the top step and listened. He was talking all the while he gave that pillow a real going-over and this is what he said.

"'You are an old meanie! You come here and take my mother to all those nice places and you don't take me!' He went on and on. He's not jealous because someone is paying attention to his mother; he is jealous because she is getting the attention he wants from this young man. Now that we know what it is, I think they can handle it, make it clear that he can go with them some of the time, but that they also want time alone."

A punching bag can be used in the preschool or at home. The children can help to make it, stuffing a pillow case or a large paper shopping bag with newspapers, old stockings — whatever is at hand.

"When my little ones are fretful we sit down and have a great time tearing up newspaper," a teacher of toddlers in a child care center related. "Then we stuff them into paper bags. I tie the end and we pretend that they are snow balls and throw them. Another time when we had filled a big bag, I hung it up and we took turns hitting it with a Nerf bat."

Tearing cloth is another way to release feelings. There is something about the sound, as well as the motion, which feels good! Joseph's teacher (Chapter 3) kept a pile of worn-out men's shirts on a shelf in a closet for this purpose. On more than one occasion Joseph vented his wrath on them! The pieces need not be thrown away. They can be used to stuff punching bags. Long strips can be used to teach braiding.

Pounding

Pounding is another means of release. In one child care center, I saw a tree stump. A small child was standing beside it pounding nails with very large heads into it. "That is our pounding place," his teacher said when she saw me looking at it. "It really makes you feel good to bang those nails with a hammer."

"What do you do when there's no room for more nails?" I asked.

"Someone takes them all out at the end of each day. It isn't as if we were destroying something they created — it's the pounding that is important."

For very little children pounding clay serves the same purpose. Before they acquire the skill for sculpture there is a lot of pounding, rolling, manipulating. I knew one teacher who, when she sensed things were getting out of hand, would quietly set up a table with clay boards and some good moist clay, and gently direct the fractious ones to it.

Painting Is More Than Art

Emotions do not always have to be expressed with violent action. Feelings can flow out, rather than erupt.

When Kevin's father was scheduled for an operation on his eye, his parents thought they had been successful in concealing their anxiety from their son.

One day his mother called the teacher. "I have a place set up in the laundry room where Kevin can play with messy materials, like clay and paint; the stuff I don't want in his room or in my kitchen. Yesterday when I was doing the wash, he was playing with his fingerpaints. He chose black and brown. I could hear him muttering, so I listened and he was saying, 'That's the gucky, mucky hospital where my dad is going!' Apparently he had heard more than we realized. We have talked it over with him, and I think he feels better now."

Helping a Child Talk Out Problems

A preschool teacher told this story of helping a child talk out his problems.

Jason's father was asked to come to the school for a conference. Jason had become very withdrawn; he was not taking part in any of the activities which he had previously enjoyed, and he rebuffed any overtures made by the teachers or children. This little boy's mother died when he was two, and after a succession of housekeepers, his father had married again.

When the director described Jason's behavior, his father said, "That certainly is different from the way he is acting at home. Instead of being quiet, he is obnoxious; interrupting when we are talking, running wildly through the house when we have company, and deliberately breaking things. He has nightmares, and has even started wetting the bed, something he stopped doing long ago."

"Could it be that he doesn't like the idea of your remarrying?" the director ventured.

"I don't think so," the father replied. "When I told him about it he seemed very happy."

The next day the teacher sat down at a low table and invited Jason to join her. Between them was a box of smooth, small, one-inch blocks. Experience had taught her that children's tongues were loosened when their hands were occupied. "Let's see what we can build with these," she said, starting to pile them up. After a few moments, Jason tentatively began to move the blocks around, feeling their smoothness, making patterns. The teacher casually brought up the subject of his new mother. "What do you call her?" she asked. Jason gradually began to talk. "I hate my new mother," he said, but his expression belied his words.

"Well, I really don't hate her, but if I get to like her she might go away like my real Mum did and like all those other ladies. They all went away." This little boy was using his second language, his behavior, to express his anxiety. When his parents understood the problem they were able to reassure him.

Water Play — the Most Accessible Material

Painting may work well in the nursery school, but all homes are not set up to accommodate the mess, and many mothers are not temperamentally suited to put up with it.

There is another soothing medium which is accessible to everyone — water! A homesick child, a lonely or shy child, an emotionally upset child, can find release standing at a sink filled with warm water — just messing around with cups, funnels, strainers, tubes or the gravy baster. Adding a handful of soapflakes will heighten the experience and a whisk is a wonderful addition.

Reading and Telling Stories

Books offer some children an outlet for the expression of their feelings. As with puppets they live vicariously through identifying with an imaginary person.

Authors like Judith Viorst write about children as they really are. When we read aloud from books like *I'll Fix Anthony,* and *Alexander and the Terrible, Horrible, No Good, Very Bad Day* we can almost feel the relief draining out of the listener.

Dorene gave Randy relief when she asked him to tell her how he felt. Making up stories can serve the same purpose. One teacher surprised the children in her classroom when she invited them to write about their feelings.

"Your story doesn't have to be about nice things. It can be about mean, scary, angry things or even about how you feel when you are doing something you know is wrong."

Some people were critical of her method. "You are encouraging bad behavior — condoning it!" they said.

"I believe that mean feelings are better put on paper than in hitting people or smashing things," was her answer.

Families can use the written word as a means of expression, also, as we saw in Philipe's poem dictated to his mother.

Music

Music is another form of therapy which can be used to release feelings. Even very young infants will respond when they are moved in time to music. The mother who dances around the room with her child in her arms, dipping, swaying, bouncing, singing, is adapting to the natural rhythm which is within the child. More than that she is conveying a sense of joy — which makes the infant feel good!

Teachers can extend this pleasure with a few simple rhythm instruments. A drum, tambourine, triangle, or a pair of cymbals can be associated with feelings. Which one would you choose to say you are angry? Which one would tell me you are happy?

Children at home often turn away from their expensive toys to play with pots and pans found in the kitchen. Two pot lids will substitute for cymbals, an aluminum or stainless steel cover will make a beautiful gong and an assortment of plastic bowls, dishpans and wastebaskets will become resounding drums.

These things I have suggested add up to fun! If you can participate in that fun you will enjoy a new relationship with your children.

Dramatic Play Discloses Feelings

The playhouse in child care centers provides a theater for acting out the problems which may be affecting a child's behavior. Teachers need to be as discreet as a priest who hears confessions, because family arguments and other intimate details are often portrayed with painful accuracy. "They're going to turn off our lights if my Dad doesn't pay the electric bill," Mary Jane announced to her friends, as proudly as if she were telling them about a party.

"Oh yeah," Roger responded. "Well we're getting a divorce! Do you have a divorce?"

If a child whacks, pinches, and slams around a doll, it is a pretty good clue as to how he really feels about the new baby at home. In this child-sized duplication of the adult world, frightening scenes, reenacted, can lose their terror.

Young children will not tell on their parents who may be physically or sexually abusing them, but a discerning teacher can gain some clues to what may be going on if she observes dramatic play. A social worker spoke to the director of a child care center. "We are taking Gina and Josephine's father to court for child abuse," she said. "Have your teachers heard or seen anything that might be used against him?"

At first, when they were asked, the teachers said that they had nothing to report except that these two little girls were abnormally quiet and withdrawn, and played only with each other. Later Lou went alone to the director. "There is something I have noticed," she said hesitantly. "Until you mentioned this, I didn't really recognize the significance of it. Every day those two little girls gather up all of the dolls and line them up on the doll's bed on their stomachs with their bottoms sticking up and their legs hanging over the edge."

A sensitive observer can get an idea of what the world looks like to a child. In most cases the teacher is not expected to interpret her observations; she should relate them to the professional who will know how to convert the child's fantasies into reality.

Another story came from the director of a day camp.

Raoul, aged seven, had his counselors, and fellow campers in a constant state of upheaval. He swore, lied, started fights deliberately and broke every rule. The director was thinking about asking his parents to withdraw him when his counselor discovered the all important key. On a rainy day he told his campers the story of the "Sorcerer's Apprentice" and played the record.

"Do you think we could make that into a show and do it for the rest of the camp?" he asked.

Raoul spoke up quickly, "I'll be the Sorcerer," he

announced. That was a turning point for this child. Raoul threw so much vigor into his part that the rest of the children were spellbound. He became a coach, director, scenery designer, and producer of this and other plays. As he found satisfaction through this and won the admiration of his pals, his whole attitude changed. He was too busy to be naughty!

Most homes have the equipment which can be assembled to create a stage for dramatic play: a small table and chairs, tea sets and discarded cookware, telephones and dress-up clothes. When a child is having a behavior problem, an ear tuned in to this corner may offer some clues.

On looking back over this chapter, I see that what I am really saying is that punishment is what we use when our adult emotions get out of hand. The suggestions offered here are ways of dealing with them before punishment is necessary.

Adages last because they condense meaning into a few easily remembered words, and certainly the time-honored saying, "An ounce of prevention is worth a pound of cure," sums up this chapter.

CHAPTER 15

A Piece of
the Action

In the business world there is a commonly used phrase, "a piece of the action." Simply stated it means that an employee who shares in the profits is motivated to work harder. This principle can be applied to the concept of discipline that *makes sense*. A family is a corporation. Adults hold the administrative positions, but when the children in a family are allowed to participate in making the rules which govern the household, they find it easier to accept them.

Bruce and Sandra Wallace found it necessary to reorganize the corporate structure of their family. Since Sandra had gone back to work they were spending too many of the precious hours they had with their children in arguments and nagging.

The Wallace Corporation — A Family Meeting

The notice on the bulletin board was impressive:
Meeting of the Wallace Corporation
July 25 at 7:30 P.M. Dining Room
"What's it all about?" Ralph asked when he came home from his school.

"I don't know any more than you do," Lola mumbled through her peanut butter and jelly sandwich.

As each of the four Wallace children read the notice, interest and curiosity mounted. When their mother came in from her job at four they plied her with questions which she answered with, "You will see."

At 7:30, with dinner over and the dishes cleared away, Bruce and Sandra sat at the head of the table, facing four attentive, expectant children.

"We have decided that it is time to let you all get involved in the business of managing a home and family," Sandra announced in serious tones. "We are going to have family meetings. With both of us working, we have to have rules about taking care of the house, and getting along with each other. Up until now we have made all those decisions — and that doesn't seem to be working very well, so now we want you to help decide what is necessary. We will start off with some basic rules.

Rule # 1: Everyone will get a chance to talk, to make suggestions, even little Jimmy.

Rule # 2: We will all listen — politely! No interruptions. No put downs, like 'stupid!' or 'that's a dumb idea!'"

"What other rules do you think we need?" Bruce asked, and was immediately barraged with heated attacks on past restrictions, everyone trying to talk at the same time.

"Stop!" said Sandra. "We can't listen when everyone talks at once. Perhaps we need to explain a little more. At Town Meetings, someone has to be a moderator, to decide who talks, and to stop people who interrupt or talk too long. The people who want to talk either stand up or raise their hands, and the moderator gives them each a turn. In our meetings, Daddy and I will be moderators. You may raise your hands. All right, Ralph, you may speak first."

"We should have bigger allowances!" Ralph got his pet peeve in first.

"I think we should be allowed to go to bed when we are ready!" Lola interjected quickly. "You always make me go when Wilma does, and I am three years older!"

"Hold it!" Bruce said. "We can talk about allowances, but Ralph, you have to understand where the money comes from. Lola, one reason you go to bed at the same time as Wilma is that you share a room."

"But that's not fair," sputtered Lola.

"Rule Number 2," cautioned Sandra. "Don't interrupt."

Lola's mutinous glare showed she didn't think much of Rule Number 2.

It isn't easy to establish a democratic procedure in a family, as Bruce was discovering. However, he recognized that part of the learning process is living with the consequences of wrong decisions. There must be flexibility. When rules are made there should be a plan for review and change. Sometimes the adult has to grit his teeth and let children learn from their mistakes.

Family meetings can serve several purposes. They can make life easier because they provide a forum for communication and reduce the need for nagging and arguments. They also can teach children the principles of democracy. However, before attempting to institute the process, parents should come to an agreement with each other about what they are trying to accomplish and how they will proceed.

It would be naive to suggest that the Wallace family meetings solved all of their problems overnight. It took several meetings, patient persistence and a determination to make it work before all of the members of the family acknowledged that it really was a good idea.

The issues they resolved come up in every family.

A suggestion on the matter of bedtime was to try letting each child decide when he would go to bed, but to insist that he must get up at the usual time the next day, and fulfill all of his expected responsibilities. Relieved of the need to rebel against parental edicts, many children will choose to go to bed earlier.

The decision on allowances depends somewhat on the parents' willingness to share the facts. If children can understand that there is just so much money to spend, and that if they receive larger allowances there may not be enough for some of the taken-for-granted luxuries, they can accept the realities.

Allowances

Connie, a single parent who was struggling to rear her three children after her husband died, decided to include her children in planning the family budget.

"Mom, I have to have sixty dollars tomorrow for a new pair of track shoes," Harry announced as he came in the back door.

"How much did you say?" Connie Martin responded from the kitchen.

"Sixty dollars," was the answer.

"Sixty dollars!" Connie shrieked. "You have to be crazy! Do you kids think I'm made of money? Have you any idea how hard I work just to put food on the table, and to buy you clothes?"

"Well I have to have them!" Harry persisted. "Coach says I can't run until I get them, and the competition is coming up next month!"

"Then let the coach buy them!" Connie answered irritably. "I haven't had a new pair of shoes for a whole year — and I am NOT going to pay sixty dollars so you can run! You'll just have to get into some other sport that isn't so expensive. Ask for a longer paper route, and get your exercise doing something useful!"

It was the end of a hard day at the office and Connie Martin was feeling sorry for herself and muttering, "The rest of the girls in the office went out to dinner together tonight and they are going to see a great show afterward. They asked me to go but I can't afford it! Instead, here I am standing over a hot stove trying to make a cheap nourishing meal look appetizing. Sure, I lost my temper, and I hate myself for it, but that kid always picks the worst possible time to come at me asking for money!"

She served up the meal in tight-lipped silence, and the children, taking their cue from her expression, ate without talking. With an eye to making amends, Connie piled generous servings of ice cream on the pie she had made over the weekend and then managed an apologetic smile.

"I'm sorry I yelled at you, Harry," she began. "I was tired and because I couldn't go out with the rest of the girls in the office, I took it out on you. I guess we can manage to find the money for the shoes.

"I wish we could find a better system," she went on. "Sometimes when you kids ask me for money I am too busy or too tired to argue, so I just give it to you and then I feel guilty and resentful. Then other times I yell at you, the way I did tonight and say 'NO' when you really need it and that makes me feel terrible.

"Now after supper I want you, Harry and Susan, to make a list of everything you can think of that you have to have money for, like bus fares and lunch money, and I am going to give you an allowance to take care of them. Then I will look at my budget and see how much I can give you for the things you couldn't plan for in advance. You will have to live within that allowance, and earn whatever you need for extras.

"I have to budget the money that I earn to buy food and pay rent, the electric, gas and phone bills, and car payments. I have to budget for the things which keep coming up like new clothes or a visit to the dentist, or something like Harry's track shoes. I think you are old enough and smart enough to learn how to manage your own budgets and if it keeps me from turning into a nagging old witch, it will be worth trying."

"Aw, you're not so bad!" Harry conceded. "But I do like the idea of an allowance. I hate having to come asking you for every little thing!"

Should an allowance be considered payment for daily chores about the home? In my opinion they are separate issues. Every member of the household who enjoys its benefits should carry some responsibility for maintaining it. They should see it as "our home" rather than a free hotel. The more they invest in that home the greater their pride will be. Making their own beds, emptying the trash, helping with the laundry and dishes should not be matters for discussion and argument. When parents offer an allowance for these simple daily tasks they are really offering a choice on something that should be taken for granted.

By the time children are old enough to have allowances, they are old enough to understand that the money earned by Mom and Dad from their jobs must first pay for necessities. What is left provides for extras, one of which may be allowances. If necessary expenses take too much, there may not be enough left for a vacation at the beach, or tickets to a ballgame, or a new video.

Why do parents find it so hard to share this kind of information with their offspring? Some feel that childhood is meant to be enjoyed, and children should not have to worry about money. Children will not worry if their parents are calm and matter-of-fact as they talk about balancing the budget.

Democracy in the Classroom

Four-year-olds are capable of participating in making rules for behavior as Mrs. Inoue, a teacher in the child care center, discovered.

It was near the end of a long cold winter and the children had been cooped up indoors more than they could tolerate. The tempo and noise level of the classroom had been steadily climbing, and Mrs. Inoue heard her own voice adding to the tumult. After a particularly hard day she went home with a severe headache, and out of desperation conceived a plan. (Note: Most teachers do not work nine to five. They do their most constructive planning when they are away from the distractions of the children.)

Arriving at school the next morning she arranged the chairs in rows, theater style.

After her father dropped her off, Gracita stood looking at the chairs in surprise.

"What is that for?" she asked. "What are we going to do? Are we having a show?"

"No," Mrs. Inoue replied. "We are having a meeting."

That was a familiar word. Parents attended meetings and sometimes teachers had to leave the classroom to go to a meeting.

Gracita took it upon herself to explain to each arrival, "We are going to have a meeting!"

Some of them sat down immediately, assuming a serious expression. When everyone was ready Mrs. Inoue called the others over, and sat down in front of them.

"Things haven't been very pleasant around here lately," she began. "I went home yesterday with a terrible headache. Does anyone know why?"

Her audience responded with giggles, solemn nods and sly grins.

"Do you know what laws are?" was her next question.

"Yeah, like don't drive too fast or you get a ticket," Mike spoke up.

"And you can't steal!" Julio interjected.

"And you shouldn't shoot people!" Emiko said with a solemn expression.

"What kind of laws could we have for our classroom?" Mrs. Inoue asked.

The answers came back thick and fast.

"Don't run indoors!"

"Don't yell!"

"Don't bump into people!"

"Don't take a toy away from someone while they are still playing with it!"

"Put the toys away after you finish playing with them!"

"Those are all good laws," Mrs. Inoue said approvingly. "Let's write them down." She printed them on a large sheet of paper and numbered them, at the same time reading each one aloud.

"Which one says don't run?" she asked.

"Number 5," Donny said, stepping up to point to it.

"Who knows what number 7 says?" was her next question.

After they played that game for awhile, she asked, "Can anyone think of another way to use these laws?"

"Well, if one kid sees another running, he could say 'Number 5!'" Sylvia said.

"Or you could just hold up four fingers and we would know it is 'Don't yell!'" Billy chimed in.

"Hey, we could put the numbers in a box, and when someone breaks a law you could tell them to go find the right number," Orlo suggested.

By the time they were through offering their ideas, most of the children had the rules very well in mind. They had learned them because they had a need and a desire to know, a basic requirement for learning and retention. This whole experiment in democracy became a good reading-readiness lesson.

The teacher who starts this democratic process early in the school year will waste less and less energy repeating and reproaching, thus leaving more time for the enjoyable aspects of teaching.

Children are quite capable of assuming far more responsibility for their own actions than we give them credit for.

On the other hand, weary, frazzled teachers who didn't get off to a good start in September may pull themselves out of a hole in January by following Mrs. Inoue's example. It is a way of making their expectations known and finding a system for restoring order to chaos.

Cassette Recorders and Message Centers

In a world where communication is a science as well as an art, there are other ways to convey messages which may have great appeal for the child who is into gadgets. With a bit of imagination the cassette player can serve this purpose.

I knew one mother who left messages on a cassette which her son listened to when he came home after school, and encouraged him to record his feelings about his day, since she couldn't be waiting with the cookies and milk and a listening ear. "A poor substitute," some will say, but it seemed to work very well in that situation. Sometimes he wiped it out after he had let off steam; sometimes he asked her to listen and on other occasions they listened together. In another family, the bulletin board was the common resource for communication. Each child looked for messages when he came home, and tacked up messages or notes of interest like "I got an A on my test!" or "I've gone to Jon's house to get some help with my math." (In a family where children have their own e-mail addresses, messages left there are another, more private communication.)

Mother took care that her messages were not all directives:

"Thank you for changing the sheets on your bed."

"Uncle Harry called and invited us to go out on his boat Sunday!"

"Get your homework done early. I have a surprise planned for tonight!"

At first glance it may seem to some readers that the idea of including children in the business of family decisions is ridiculous. What it really adds up to is treating children like intelligent human beings. We need to remind ourselves that we do not own them, they are loaned to us. If someone gives you temporary custody of a cherished treasure, you are expected to return it in at least as good condition as you received it.

When we are dealing with the lives of young children, our obligation extends far beyond that.

CHAPTER 16

Wrong Way! Turn Back!

Not long ago as I was driving on a major highway, I allowed myself to get too preoccupied with thoughts for this book and suddenly found myself facing the sign: **WRONG WAY! TURN BACK!** Traffic was not heavy at the time and I was able to extricate myself from the problem without too much difficulty. How nice it would have been, I thought, if I could have encountered some similar warning signs when I was bringing up my children!

If you have read this far, you have probably recognized yourself on some of the preceding pages. Did you like what you saw? When I made my mistake on the highway, I had no options, I had to back down and take a different road. As a parent or teacher you have a choice. You can stiffen your back and state unequivocally, "I don't *need* this! All this talk about feelings and letting off steam is just more of that permissive stuff! I just want my kids to be decent, law abiding, God-fearing citizens, who respect their elders, and that means they have to learn to do what they are told!"

On the other hand, you might say in a more reflective manner, "I really love my kids, but no one would ever believe that if they heard me yelling at them. I try to do what is best for them but when I discipline them, I feel like a tyrant. The books all say I should be enjoying them, but just when I try to be nice and have a little fun, they do some crazy thing that makes me mad and we are enemies again. I'd like to change directions, but how do I begin?"

A Plan for Change

You have taken the first step when you recognize that behavior problems are never black or white, right or wrong, but stem from a mixture of people, environment and circumstances. The part of parenting called "Discipline" is a learned skill, and there are plenty of "experts" eager to help you. Your newspapers, magazines, radio and T.V. offer a smorgasbord of advice. Out of that rich, and sometimes indigestible, fare you can select that which seems palatable. What you retain and digest will become your own personal philosophy for child rearing. You will know it is right because it will "set well." You can never follow exactly in the footsteps of a Dr. T. Berry Brazelton, or psycholgists on television — or even a Dr. Grace Mitchell. You take something from each one and build your own composite. The key is to have an open mind, listen, observe, sift the evidence and draw your own conclusions. Games have always been popular, not just for children but for the whole family. That same problem-solving energy can be applied to the fascinating challenge of discipline. Unlike the Rubik's cube, there is no absolute final solution when you are dealing with people relationships, but there is always another chance.

Look at Your Own I AM

I was asked, "Would you do anything different if you were bringing up children today?" That was an intriguing thought. My response had to begin with "How am I different?" It was very plain that the greatest change in my attitudes, and in my own self-development, came when I absorbed the I AM! I CAN! concept.

With that as my guide, I know that if I were "parenting" now I would be able to look at the causes of behavior rather than the deeds; that I would read the messages my children were conveying in their own language. My goals would be different because I would be more concerned about helping them to develop a strong I AM than with having them become models of good behavior who would reflect credit on me.

If you asked me where to begin on a plan for changing your direction, I would have to say, "With your own self-concept." Putting modesty aside, and knowing that your list will never be scrutinized or graded, make up a balance sheet of your strengths and your weaknesses. For example:

| I yell a lot | *but* | We do have some good laughs together. |
| I make my kids obey the rules | *but* | They always know what the rules are. |

This gives you something concrete to work on. Once you have acknowledged your weaknesses, you can tackle them, one at a time. Don't expect to change overnight. Nibble away at them, and someday you will realize that you have taken a big bite!

How Were You Disciplined?

The next step to think about is the way you were treated when you were growing up. Were your parents too harsh? Too lenient? How were you disciplined? Did it accomplish the best results? Were you left filled with resentment, promising yourself never to treat your children that way? How well do you adhere to that resolve now? We have a tendency to perpetuate the mistakes of those who went before us. Are you spanking, yelling, shaming, piling guilt on your kids because that is what was done to you? Or have you gone to the other extreme, being overly indulgent, subconsciously trying to even the score?

If you are a teacher, think back through the years of your schooling. How many of your teachers left a clear impression on you? How many can you name? Are you surprised to find how few come clearly to mind? If your memories are strong, was it because they were a good influence or so mean that you still get a tight feeling inside when you think about them? Are your fondest recollections of teachers who ran a tight ship, who made their expectations clear and enforced the rules?

My husband, a high school teacher for many years, had a

reputation for being very strict. I'm sure the students referred to him as "Old Man Mitchell" and worse. Nevertheless, people came up to him at social gatherings and said, "You won't remember me, but I had you for a teacher at Newton High. I thought you were pretty mean and tough, but I learned more from you than any other teacher I ever had. I didn't dare try any funny business, but you were always fair."

It saddens me when I see teachers in child care who seem to have their notions of discipline encased in cement. "Get in line!" "Sit still!" "Apologize!" "Be quiet!!!" "When will you grow up?" and I can easily visualize the teachers who taught them.

I am reminded of a phrase I once heard: "Teachers of young children take the wriggling, squirming little humans in their care and manipulate all the joy out of their lives!"

When you have passed through the first stage, reaffirming your own I AM, you will be able to acknowledge that you are making the mistake of carrying on with someone else's methods, and shift into your own teaching style.

What Kind of Adults Do You Want Your Children to Be?

What kind of people will be the best guardians of our future? Will the way we treat our children produce the results we want?

I suggest that you refer once more to the definition, which I believe is the cornerstone of positive disciplinary practices.

Discipline is the slow, bit-by-bit, time consuming task of helping children see the sense in acting a certain way.

It points the way to self-discipline, and a person who is in control of herself is a self confident, competent individual who knows who she is, where she wants to go, and how to get there. Remember, helping a child is an investment, and the rewards will come when you receive the interest. When my children were old enough to do extraordinary things for me and I expressed my gratitude, they answered, "Just the interest on your investment!"

And if you do decide to make that kind of an investment, how will you know when you are making progress? When the day comes that you can step into the skin of the child who is antagonizing you; when you can concentrate on the "why" of her behavior, rather than the deed itself, it is as if some magical process takes over. You reach a new level of maturity and self-confidence. Like all real magic it is difficult to explain, but when it happens to you, you will know it!

It's Later Than You Think!

It can't stop there. Don't ever think you have it made. You will need to keep up your strength and continued growth with what I call educational vitamins. Attend a lecture or a workshop, read a new book or reread an old one with a new perspective. Keep your viewpoint fresh and your mind open, and enjoy your children. It's later than you think!

CHAPTER **17**

In a Nutshell

I have presented many ideas in this book, any one of which could be a subject for discussion. To summarize, let me extract from them a few "pearls of wisdom" which are so basic that the reader might shrug and say, "Of course! Anyone knows that!" They bear repeating.

If each of these rules were practiced, parents and teachers would find their lives easier, and children could enjoy their childhood years.

1. Start a planned program for discipline at a very early age. The years before six are the best years for learning. Problems which develop then can be resolved as easily as pulling out a long basting thread. Trying to help a child of seven or eight who is already messed up is more like picking at the tiny threads of machine stitching.

2. Find something to love in every child. I know it is hard if he is dirty, smelly, swears at you or hits you, but it is your job to keep trying.

3. Make certain that every child finds some small measure of success every day and praise him for it. It may be, "I see that you are trying to remember to close the door quietly," but he needs encouragement if his I AM is going to feed his I CAN and keep that wheel spinning in a positive direction.

4. Be fair and consistent. Weaving back and forth pulls the rug out from under a child's feet. If it is right today and wrong

145

tomorrow; if he is smothered with love at one moment and severely punished the next without understanding what he may have done to deserve it, life becomes very confusing. The scars left on his developing personality may never heal.

5. Avoid labeling. "The child becomes what he sees in your eyes!" If you constantly tell him that he is "stupid," a "slow-poke," "sneaky," "a liar," or a "mean kid," you will find him fitting that label.

6. Parents and teachers, cooperate. You have a common goal. Teachers can share what they have learned from working with large numbers of children, but only the parents know about all of the factors which come together to make their child unique.

Have faith in each other. Trust and respect each other, and the child will be the winner.

Index

Adjustment
  to work environment, 117
  to new baby, 74–75
  when new baby becomes "cute",
    76–77
Admitting mistakes
  child, 86–87
  parent, 104
  teacher, 85
Allowances, 133
Anticipate
  as a teacher, 6, 7
  before arrival of new baby, 75,
    79–80
  parents, to avoid problems, 10–11
  when mother is child's teacher,
    108–110
Apologies
  demanding, 92–93
  mouthing, 93–94
  parent to child, 93
  child to teacher, 93–95
  teacher to class, 15
Approval
  child's need for, 36, 116
Arguing
  children with parents, 50
  when to just say "no", 96

Bedtime
  a reasonable solution, 131
  rules for, 49
Behavior
  as second language, 25, 31
  biting, 54
  clues to, 17–20
  regressive, 81, 107-108, 124
Biting, 53–56
  age differences, 54
  because of sibling jealousy, 75
  never bite back, 56
  seeking clues through observation,
    21
  supervision to prevent, 55–56, 76
Books and stories
  as outlet for expression of feelings,
    125

before arrival of new baby, 80
  in teaching value of truth, 60–61
Bribes
  are like blackmail, 91
  for eating, 43
Bulletin board
  to improve communicatiion, 136
Buying time, 14, 15

Cassette players
  to improve communication, 136
Change, 140–141
Child abuse
  clues seen in dramatic play, 127
  emotional, 35
  spanking without self-control, 105
  verbal, 103, 105-106
Choices
  implied in threats, 85
  living with wrong choice, 87
  offering opportunities for, 86
Clay
  as means of releasing hostility, 123
Communication
  caregivers to infants, 25, 26
  child's confusion over meanings,
    23–24
  child's second language, 31
  first step is to listen, 24
  home to school, 31
  in family meetings, 130–131
  parent to child, 30–31
  positive directions, 26
  problem for working parents, 136
  spoken word best tool, 25
  teacher to parent, 9–11, 54–58
  with child about biting, 55
  with parents about biting, 55
Comparisons, 89–90
Competition, 90
Confrontation
  child with teacher, 13, 26
  over eating, 42
  over natural routines, 41
Consistency
  adults find hard to maintain, 36
  basic rule, 145

dealing with temper, 70
how to achieve, 36
in rules for bedtime, 48, 49
key to behavior management, 11
lack of destroys trust, 33
Courtesy
parent for child, 36, 44
Curriculum, 51

Decision making
important training, 86
Definition (of discipline), 3, 142
cornerstone of discipline, 142
biting, 56
feelings, 115
lying, 60
obscenity, 63
meetings, 129
on prevention of problems, 115
on punishment, 103
Democracy
in classrooms, 134–135
in family, 129–133
Development
ages and stages, 100
reasonable expectations, 18
teachers can help parents, 78
Diary, (journal) 100
Dictating
child's letter, 78
to relieve feelings, 117–119
Discipline
and parenting, 140
child can accept when fair, 112, 142
common ideas of, 2
definition of, 3, 142
for obscenity, 65
parents create own problems, 83
self-discipline, 3, 39
stems from own experience, 141
Diversionary tactics
for screaming, 68–69
for throwing things, 67
Dramatic play
as means of improving behavior 128
discloses children's feelings, 126–127
in the home environment, 128
Dressing
letting child do it, 50

Eating
in group, 45
in home, 42–43
Eliminating (toileting)
consider age, 46
when it becomes a problem, 47, 48
Environment
cause of behavior, 18–19
in center, 10
for eating, 43–44
in home, 21–22, 51
Expectations
based on own experience, 141
grandparents of child, 120

Feelings
and attitudes toward obscenity, 64–65
anger, ways to control, 13–14, 15
caused by biting, 53
child left to handle alone, 111
fear, child's reaction to, 29, 30
helping child to recognize, 115
jealousy of new baby, 73–74, 78, 81
legitimate means of releasing, 68, 118, 119, 121–122, 123, 124, 125, 126
of working parents, 99
parents have right to, 34
recognizing child's, 15, 30, 40, 143
repressing, 71, 78, 115
school age write about, 125
the "put down", 88–89
Frank, Dr. Lawrence, 38
Frustration
in child, caused by teacher, 116
of parent, 9
of single, working parent, 131–132
when teacher has own child in class, 108

Guilt
of working parents, 100, 132
parents, 34
piling on child, 141

Hesitate, 3, 14, 30, 105

I AM, I CAN
a philosophy that works, 1–2
a basic rule for success, 145

first step toward change, 140–142
for positive reinforcement,
115–116
putting it into reverse, 2, 90, 116
Investigate
before blaming, 28–30
before making accusations, 57-58
people problems, 18
when child bites, 54–55
when toileting is a problem, 46–47
Isolation
when a child bites, 55

Jealousy
child of mother's boyfriend, 122
covering up, 78
delayed feelings of, 77-78
of child when mother is a teacher,
107–108
of new baby, 73
parents' solution, 75, 76–77
Jumping to conclusions
about child's behavior, 121
pertaining to lying, 56–58

Language
age differences, 23, 25-26
bathroom talk, 65–66
behavior is second, 25, 31
cultural practices, 63-64
gives sense of power, 26
giving the child words to use,
63–64
unacceptable, 62, 64–65
Lear, Edward
Nonsense Alphabet, 65–66
Learning
continual process, 6–7
early years crucial, 145
start where learner is, 63
to live with wrong decisions, 87,
131
Linkletter, Art, 87
Listening
honest listening, 24
to cassette player, 136
Love
key to trust, 35
something in every child, 145
Lying
adults set pattern, 59–60
causes, 61
to avoid punishment, 60
versus imagination, 57
When is it a lie?, 59

Manners
at meals, 44
Meetings
family, 129–131
in classroom, 134–135
Montessori method
sense of order, 52
Music, 126

Nagging, 43, 95–96
Name calling, 39, 146
New baby
jealousy of, 73
preparing child in advance, 75

Observation
keeping a journal, 100
Order
as it leads to learning, 52
system for, 52

Painting
as means of expression, 123, 124
Parent abuse, 70
Parent-teacher relationships
about biting, 55
helping parent anticipate
problems, 10-11
need to understand each other, 99,
101
teacher with working parents, 99
Permissiveness
causes child anxiety, 42
Planning
by teacher, 7, 134
children share in, 75, 135
in anticipation of new baby, 79–81
program for discipline, 145
Poetry
child uses to express feelings,
117–118
Positive direction
director to staff, 99–100
teacher to child, 26
Positive reinforcement, 70–71,
115–116

Pounding
  as means of releasing hostility,
    122, 123
Praise
  as a reward, 11
  earned, 91, 92
  for helping with new baby, 80
  for table manners, 44
  when child exerts self-control, 70
Pressure cooker, 117
Problem solving
  child to child, 26–28
  parent needs imagination, 105
Program, 19–21
Punching bag
  as means of releasing hostility,
    121–122
Punishment
  children can accept if fair, 112
  for lying, 60
  form of aggression, 36
  if inconsistent, unfair, 36
  relieves adult frustration, 104,
    128
  to fit the crime, 90, 112
Puppets
  as means of expression, 119

Quiet places
  where child can be alone, 19, 111

Reading readiness
  an example of, 135
Reading stories
  in preparing for new baby, 80
  in relation to lying, 60–61
  to help express feelings, 125
Referrals
  about toileting, 46–47
Regression
  wetting bed, 108, 124
  when new baby comes, 81
Rejection
  of child, when mother is her
    teacher, 107
Resources
  people to call on, 101
Respect
  key to trust, 35
  parents and teachers for each
    other, 146

Responsibility
  children in classrooms, 136
  children in home, 133
  for helping with baby, 80
  never-ending for parents, 10
  parents for children, 137
Rewards
  after earned, 91
  for eating, 43
  gold stars, 91
  praise for helping, 11
Riley, Sue Spayth, 85
Role model
  adult displaying temper, 69–70
  adults set tone of behavior, 116
  in use of unacceptable language,
    62–63, 65
  lying before child, 59–60
  parent teaches honesty, 62
  teacher, 13–14
Rules
  children help make, 135
  for bedtime, 49
  for eating, 44, 45
  for games involving throwing, 67
  for parents and teachers,
    145–146
  involving family meetings, 130
  plan for review and change, 131
  set ground rules, 36

Safety
  in play, 67
Scolding
  parents after bad report from
    teacher, 99
  when parent has own child in
    class, 107
Screaming
  diversionary tactics, 68–69
Security
  comes from adults, 40, 96
  through consistency, 11
Self-confidence, 1, 142
Self-control
  in teacher, 13
  lack of in adult, 38, 105
  lack in child, 111
  suggestions to help child, 14–15
  teaching child importance of, 94
Self-discipline, 142

Sense of humor
  in time of crisis, 15, 85
Separation
  as punishment, 110–112
Setting limits
  children need, 96
  for choices, 86
  for punishment, 112
Skills for daily living
  part of curriculum, 51
Sleeping
  child who goes into parents' bed,
    49–50
  naptime in center, 41–42
  rules for bedtime at home, 49
  wandering through house at night,
    50
Spanking, 103–105
Stealing
  age related, 61
  parent teaches honesty by
    example, 62
Supervision
  teacher by supervisor, 97–99
  when a child bites, 55–56
Support
  call in reserves, 101
  day care supports parents, 101
  director to teacher, 101
  parent for child, 70
  supervisor to director, 97–100

Talk-it-over chairs, 26–28
Tearing
  as means of releasing hostility, 122
Temper tantrums
  different kinds, 69
  Joseph, 13–14

Thinking chair, 111
Threats
  over eating, 43
  you can't carry out, 84
  that imply a choice, 85
Throwing
  child, to relieve feelings, 119
  child, unintentionally hitting
    another, 67
  legitimate uses of, 67
  with intent to hurt, 68
Time
  child's sense of, 73, 111
  giving child time to learn, 50
"Time out", 111
Toy chests, 52
Transition
  from one activity to another, 7–8
Trust
  adults can destroy, 33
  and lying, 60
  begins at birth, 34
  child, of adult, 24
  How do we instill?, 35

Values
  adults — lying, 59–60
  brought from home, 63
Viorst, Judith, 125

Water play
  to relieve tension, 125
Working parents
  and communication, 136
  and family meetings, 129–131
  anxiety, 99
  in a child care center, 108–110
  problems of, 36

About the Author

Dr. Grace Mitchell is an author, lecturer, consultant, and co-founder of a national chain of child care centers. A pioneer in the field of early childhood education, she has authored six books on child care and preschool curriculum based upon her I AM! I CAN! philosophy. Dr. Mitchell earned her Ed.M. from Harvard University and her Ph.D. from The Union Institute.

"*A Very Practical Guide to Discipline* may sound like a guide to punishment, but it is actually a guide to avoiding punishment. Although she encourages parents to find ways to avoid problem situations, she states that there are times when punishment is necessary. When a child infringes on the rights of another person, by hurting them or destroying property, or being deliberately rude, penalties are in order.

"The lynchpin of Mitchell's philosophy is "I AM, I CAN," which encourages self-esteem in children on the theory that an individual with a healthy self-image is better able to function in society.

"Mitchell draws on her five decades as a parent, grandparent, teacher and school administrator to look at the issues that parents face every day. She uses scores of based-on-fact anecdotes to describe the techniques she has developed for handling age-old problems. The stories she tells are sometimes humorous, sometimes sad, always insightful."

> Christine McKenna
> Lowell Sun, Lowell, Mass.

"In an easy-to-read style, Mitchell outlines her four point plan of action: Anticipate, Hesitate, Investigate and Communicate. This and her I AM, I CAN philosophy have become measuring sticks for child-rearing."

> C. J. Boyer
> Las Vegas Review-Journal

"Mitchell is very much in touch with today's young children, and has a warm writing style that makes *A Very Practical Guide to Discipline* easy to read."

> Marge Cocker
> Seattle Post-Intelligencer

"A good-natured, commonsensical approach to the age-old problems of child-rearing, distilled from better than fifty years of dealing with kids."

> Jerry Carroll
> San Francisco Chronicle

"The Mitchell book is briskly written, replete with sound advice and anecdotes which help clarify and illuminate her message."

> Larry Rumley
> Seattle Times

"Dr Mitchell's book offers a variety of down to earth techniques as a source for both parents and teachers to use while they are guiding and nurturing the lives of young children. Every school in our company has one."

> Buffy Owens
> Executive Vice President
> Palo Alto Preschools

"Dr Mitchell doesn't preach or make us feel guilty about the mistakes we've all made with our children. Instead, true to life situations help us to really understand how positive discipline works.

"Anticipate, Hesitate, Investigate, Communicate is a plan of action that will work for parents and teachers. It will allow us, bit by bit, to develop in children the ability to be responsible for their own behavior."

> Judith Adorno
> Region Manager
> Kindercare Learning Centers

"This is an ideal book for child care teachers as well as parents. Dr. Mitchell, through many lively anecdotes gives the reader an understanding of what makes children tick. There is no simple formula or recipe for discipline. Instead, she offers flexible techniques that work. At last, a book on discipline that makes sense."

> Karen Miller
> Director of Training
> Children's World